Critic

Dreaming Bears

"We won't be seeing stories like this anymore, this remarkable real-deal first-person account of two generous and wry Indian elders who were still living out in the Brooks Range wilderness in the 1960s. Johnny and Sarah Frank's memories reach back to the time before settled villages, to years of near-starvation and animal dreaming, while their grandchildren would become Native leaders in the modern era. Their story is told by a wide-eyed Southern doctor who stumbles into the Chandalar River country and is transformed into an advocate for the protection of wild Alaska and Native subsistence rights."

—Tom Kizzia
Author of *Pilgrim's Wilderness* and *The Wake of the Unseen Object*

"The fight to save the calving grounds of the caribou in the Arctic National Wildlife Refuge is one of the great environmental issues of our time. It is also a fight to save the Gwich'in—the northernmost Indians in North America—who depend on the caribou to sustain their way of life which has existed since time immemorial. Mike Holloway's book based on his experiences with an elderly Gwich'in couple illuminates the Gwich'in way of life and provides the reader with an understanding on why both the caribou and the Gwich'in need to be saved."

—John E. Echohawk,
Executive Director, Native American Rights Fund

"A well-told, straightforward tale that rings absolutely true. *Dreaming Bears* is reality, not romance—albeit a reality that many a romantic would envy! Through the shape of other lives and the arc of their stories, we learn about the world; reading Holloway is like a long talk around the campfire with a new friend."

—Sharman Apt Russell
Author of *Standing in the Light: My Life as a Pantheist*
and *Hunger: An Unnatural History*

"The next best thing to hunting bear (among other animals) at 55 degrees below zero above the Arctic Circle with an elderly Alaskan Gwich'in named Johnny Frank may be to read about it, and much more, in J. Michael Holloway's captivating *Dreaming Bears*. In ways a coming of age journey, *Dreaming Bears* is even more an unfolding love letter from a non-Native doctor to Johnny and Sarah Frank, their extended Gwich'in family, and to their talents for survival, not to mention generosity. Johnny is the lodestar, a man who mixes Biblical and Gwich'in stories between an obligation to wrest any and every kind of meat from the snow and tundra, and to find patience in existence."

—Alison Owings
Author of *Indian Voices: Listening to Native Americans*

Dreaming Bears

A GWICH'IN INDIAN STORYTELLER,
A SOUTHERN DOCTOR,
A WILD CORNER OF ALASKA

J. Michael Holloway

Epicenter Press

Epicenter Press
6524 NE 181st Street #2
Kenmore, WA 98028
(425) 485-6822
www.epicenterpress.com

Epicenter Press is a regional press publishing nonfiction books about the arts, history, environment, and diverse cultures and lifestyles of Alaska and the Pacific Northwest.

Cover photo and maps by Margie Ann Gibson

ISBN 978-1-935347-30-9

Library of Congress Control Number: 2014933733

10 9 8 7 6 5 4 3 2 1

Printed in Canada
Printed on post-consumer recycled paper

Dedication

This book is dedicated with love to my friend, companion and wife, Margie Gibson.

Table of Contents

Foreword

This is a powerful story of friendship and a deep love of nature that transformed lives and altered the fate of an Indian nation.

When young Mike Holloway took a break from his medical studies for a summer of backpacking in Alaska he had no way of knowing he was about to forge a bond with a traditional medicine man—let alone play a pivotal role at the most critical moment in the history of the Gwich'in, the northernmost American Indians in the world.

It all began with a misadventure. Mike made it to the remote village of Venetie, but his idea of simply heading out across country, as he might in his native South Carolina, proved unrealistic. What to do?

"Well," said the chief of Venetie, "Better for you to go up to Gold Camp on East Fork, see Johnny Frank." So he did, arriving exhausted after a 36-mile hike to find Johnny and Sarah, already in their eighties, living quietly by themselves, hunting and fishing much as their people had for thousands of years.

Sitting around a campfire with Johnny, Mike saw that the Gwich'in had been content to live quietly in their corner of the world, letting the commotion of the twentieth century pass them by. There were no roads to their villages. It was fine with them if few from the outside world visited—or even knew they existed.

At summer's end, Mike returned to medical school. In time, he became a highly skilled orthopedic surgeon and moved to Alaska. Though he began raising a family near Anchorage, he got out to see Johnny and Sarah whenever he could. With each visit, Mike grew closer to them and learned more about the Gwich'in.

Much as the Plains Indians once depended on buffalo, the Gwich'in still depend on caribou. Artifacts indicate that caribou and ancestral Gwich'in have shared this part of the Arctic for at least 27,000 years. Elders like Johnny Frank may not count the years, but they say their relationship with the caribou began long ago, in a time when all creatures spoke the same language. In that distant time the caribou and the people were one. As they evolved into separate beings, the tundra sustained the caribou and the caribou sustained the Gwich'in. Mike was among the first to see that this relationship with the caribou might suddenly end —and if it did, the Gwich'in way of life would collapse.

Oil companies had already developed the huge Prudhoe Bay field and now wanted to move into the Arctic National Wildlife Refuge to drill in the heart of caribou calving grounds. Mike alerted the Gwich'in, who immediately understood that if there was drilling in their calving grounds the caribou would go the way of the buffalo. Political forces were aligned to open the refuge to drilling. The Gwich'in had to act immediately.

Act they did, traveling to Washington, D.C., again and again, to convince lawmakers that the Arctic Coastal Plain had to remain closed to drilling to protect both the Porcupine caribou herd and the Gwich'in. Mike worked tirelessly with the Gwich'in, even taking a leave of absence from his medical work to lobby in Washington D.C.

It's been a joy to see Mike honored by the Gwich'in and by his peers in the medical profession. It's been inspiring to see how he's fought for others over the years. Now, it's a great joy to see that Mike has written such a beautiful and moving account of his friendship with Johnny and Sarah.

Alaska is often called The Last Frontier. Viewed as a man of this frontier, Mike Holloway is, in his own way, as important as Kit Carson, the renowned mountain man, was in his day. They both went out to the margins of civilization and the wilderness. They both encountered Native Americans who had a great desire to live as their ancestors had lived. Unlike Carson, who helped usher in the demise of Indians by killing the wild creatures they depended on, Mike devoted himself to protecting both the animals and the people.

Among the Gwich'in, Mike Holloway will be remembered as "The Messenger."

For all of us, it's heartening to know that the history of the American frontier, which saw the devastation of so many creatures and Native cultures, includes a Mike Holloway whose vision and sensibilities helped preserve rather than destroy. And it all started with a young man's desire to head out for Alaska.

—Art Davidson
author of the classic *Minus 148 Degrees: The First Winter Ascent of Mt. McKinley*

Introduction

The Athabascan Gwich'in people, the northernmost Indians in North America, live in remote villages scattered across the vast interior Arctic. In northeast Alaska, their traditional homeland extends from the Chandalar River in the west, across the river valleys draining southern slopes of the Brooks Range, and eastward into northwest Canada as far as the Arctic Red River, a tributary to the Mackenzie.

The Gwich'in refer to themselves as caribou people, as they rely for their survival on a caribou herd named for the Porcupine River, which flows into the Yukon. They feel a spiritual connection to the caribou.

For thousands of years, Gwich'in roamed the slopes of the lofty mountains, down the rivers through forested hill country into the marshy Yukon Flats. Traditionally the people traveled in small nomadic bands seeking food, in a land where winters were long and bitterly cold, and summers hot and buggy. The people did not accumulate material goods. By necessity they traveled with the absolute basics. The Gwich'in were masters in the art of survival.

I knew little of this in 1961 when I set out from South Carolina with my brother and a college friend to spend a summer hiking into the remote, roadless Arctic. What began as a wilderness camping trip became another thing altogether. The tribal chief of the Venetie Indian Reservation directed us to the remote home of Johnny and Sarah Frank, an elderly Gwich'in couple who still lived off the land, forty miles from the closest village and a hundred miles from the closest road.

Johnny, a well-known storyteller among his people, described himself as a former medicine man. He dreamed of bears. Johnny and Sarah were to become my mentors, my adoptive grandparents, the godparents of my son. Their wisdom and generosity would shape the rest of my life.

Near the end of Johnny's life, I tried to articulate how lucky I was to have met him and Sarah. Johnny only replied, "Not luck."

This is our story.

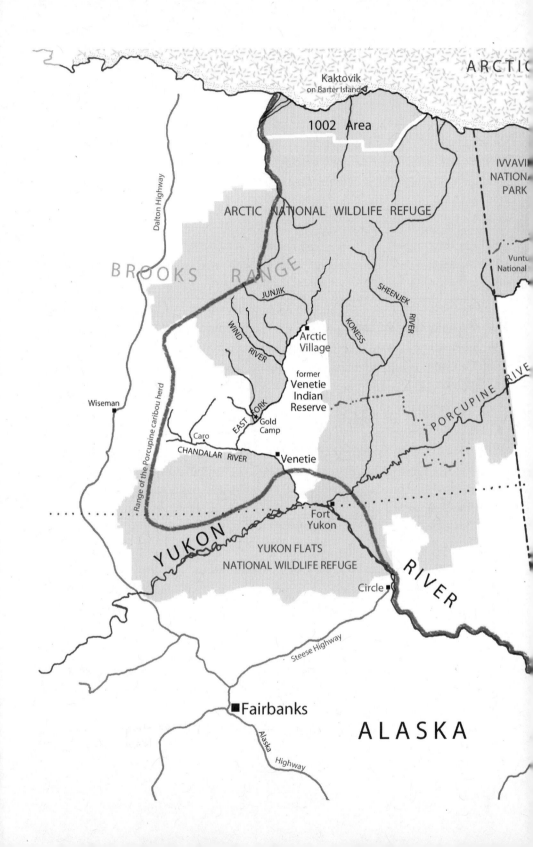

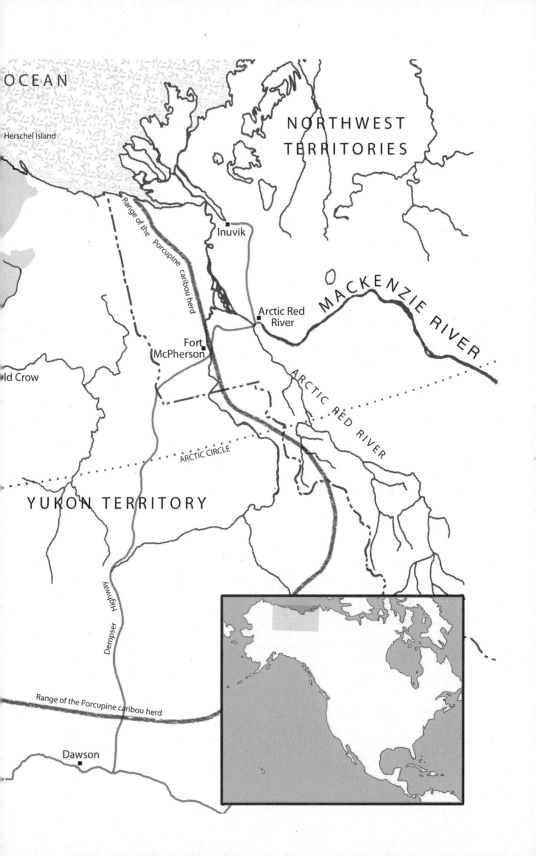

OCEAN

Herschel Island

NORTHWEST
TERRITORIES

Range of the Porcupine caribou herd

Inuvik

MACKENZIE RIVER

Arctic Red
River

Fort
McPherson

ARCTIC RED RIVER

Old Crow

ARCTIC CIRCLE

YUKON TERRITORY

Dempser Highway

Range of the Porcupine caribou herd

Dawson

CHAPTER 1

Medical School

Crossing the dorm room quietly, I lowered a stack of anatomy books to my bed, then turned to wash my hands of the formaldehyde embalming mixture that freshmen medical students reeked with after cadaver dissection. This awakened my roommate, Don Rhame.

"Your father called. He wants you to call back tonight."

"Did he mention why?"

"No, but he said it wasn't an emergency."

As I dried my hands, I grinned at Don lying on his bed, a huge textbook opened over his chest. This was a sure way of getting a nap.

"Did you get any studying done?"

"Not much," he yawned.

It seemed futile to study these last few days before final exams. The volume of material was too immense to review but tension drove us to study anyway. In no subject were we given enough information to know whether we were passing or failing. These exams in May 1961 would bring to a close our freshman year at the Medical College of South Carolina in Charleston. We knew a few of us would have to retake a course, perhaps two, during the summer. I did not want to be among them. I had other plans.

I called collect from the pay phone down the hall. Pop accepted the charges.

"Mike, how are things?" He had finished medical school in Charleston some twenty-five years before.

"Pretty good. Trying to study."

"Listen. Teddy hasn't got a summer job. The mill is laying off and can't use summer help. When I was bird hunting last week, the jeep threw a rod. Mister Hammond in Newberry is overhauling the engine. If you include Teddy in your plans, you can take the jeep to Alaska."

My mind reeled. My younger brother, Ted, a gangly sixteen-year-old, was still in high school. Bill Bennett and I were leaving around the first of June, ten days away. We had planned to hitchhike approximately four thousand miles to Alaska.

"Well, think about it and let me know," Pop said, irritated by my silence.

"Yes sir. I appreciate the offer. It's just sudden. I need to think about it and talk to Bill."

"Call when you decide."

In spite of our age difference, my brother Ted and I had spent a lot of time together. Like me, he had short, dark brown hair and brown eyes, but already was an inch taller. Having grown up fishing and hunting with our father, we were comfortable with firearms and knew how to handle them safely. Ted was a good driver and a hard worker. He was easy going and had a knack of manipulating his two older brothers into frequent quarrels. Mother thought Teddy was a little angel until surgery restored her hearing. Then she could hear not only the buzzing of bees again but Teddy's softly spoken quips as well.

I went to Bill's room. He was propped on pillows reading notes. He threw them aside as I entered, ready to talk about Alaska. His face fell as I explained Pop's offer of the jeep.

"It'll cost too much! We don't have enough money to drive." Bill was a master of traveling on limited funds. He had taken a break from college and traveled alone by freighter, arriving in Scotland with shirt and tie, overcoat and oxfords, carrying a suitcase. Fifteen months later he returned thin and poor with bedraggled clothes but mentally strong and independent.

"But we won't get stuck in cities on our way to Alaska," I argued, though not convinced myself. "We could camp where we want, stop when we want. If the jeep held up, we might do all right. There would be three ways to share expenses!"

I had doubts. Three of us crowded into the jeep? My kid brother? Bill and I had planned this trip for months. The idea took hold in January when Bill went with me to the Charleston docks, where I was determined to get seaman's papers and a freighter job that would take me back to Europe. I had been there two years before at age nineteen. When a job in Germany fell through, I'd stayed in youth hostels and learned to live inexpensively. Frightened at first, I became comfortable being on my own and found helpful people throughout my travels.

I loved to travel. Born in Greenwood, South Carolina, in 1940, I had made two roundtrips to the Pacific Coast by age five. During World War II, we moved around with my father to his U.S. Navy assignments until he shipped out for the invasion of Iwo Jima as a combat surgeon with the Marine Corps.

After the war, we settled in a small mill town in upper South Carolina. The South was a racially segregated society and remained so for the next twenty-five years. South Carolina was the first state to secede from the Union and the last to re-enter it after the Civil War. We are a proud and hotheaded people with a tendency to offend too easily. I have heard it said that South Carolina is too small to be a country but too large to be an insane asylum.

My great grandfathers were teenage soldiers in the Confederate Army and fought valiantly against the invasion of their homeland. My ancestors fought in the Revolutionary War and the Mexican War. Proud of this family history, I had attended The Citadel, the Military College of South Carolina.

On the Charleston waterfront that gray, rainy winter day a few months before, I had been unable to get a ship captain's signature, which was needed to get seaman's papers. Soon Bill Bennett and I were browsing in a warm, dry bookstore on lower King Street, buying books on Alaska.

I don't believe we ever decided to go, not in any formal way. Between Bill's enthusiasm and my desire to visit a natural land undisturbed by humans we came around to the idea of a summer adventure in the far north. We read about Alaska, ordered books and maps, combed through libraries, and talked endlessly about when, how, and where we would explore the new state.

Bill believed that in ten weeks or so we could hike from the end of the road system at Circle City on the Yukon River across the Arctic wilderness to Barrow, Alaska's northernmost settlement. I was not so sure. It became evident that this plan was not practical as I examined topographical maps and reviewed geographic surveys of the Brooks Range and North Slope. Reading *Arctic Wilderness* by Robert Marshall, who wrote about his travels in the central Brooks Range around 1930, convinced me that overland travel by foot in the summer would be slow and tedious, through difficult terrain with mosquitoes in great abundance. The country seemed far different from the mountains of northern New Mexico where, at sixteen, I had once walked two hundred miles in two weeks. We scaled back our plans. We would hitchhike as far north as we could by road and then continue on foot, flying back at the end of the summer from the farthest-north village we could reach.

Pop's call might force another change in our plans. How well did I know Ted? Did I want family along on this venture? I had lots of questions.

"It will cost too much," Bill insisted.

"Let's think it over, do some calculations."

Returning to my room, I explained the situation to Don. He considered Bill and me to be a bit off, but thought that taking the jeep instead of hitchhiking across the continent would restore a measure of sanity to our summer plans. I settled down to study but soon drifted off. Later, my fatigue gone, I stayed up until dawn studying maps and roughing out the cost of gasoline.

I decided to take the jeep. Bill would wait for grades, which were to be mailed around June 10. If he passed, he would hitchhike. We agreed to meet in Fairbanks no later than June 21—a tight schedule for Bill.

A former classmate from Pittsburgh, Richard Volkwein, had been thinking about hitchhiking to Alaska with Bill and me. Volk, as I called him, was about to graduate from The Citadel, Class of 1961. We had been classmates in the same rifle company there for three years before I began medical school. Volk and I had become friends, kidding one another about him being a Yankee and me being a Rebel.

Volk's father, like mine, was a family medical doctor. Volk was thin-framed with brown hair and dark eyes. Cadets at The Citadel were assigned companies by height; we were both five-foot-seven, so we ended up together in H Company. As freshmen plebes, we endured the harassment that comes with the first year of military school as one-third of our classmates dropped out.

Volk and I were corporals our junior year, in charge of disciplining freshmen. We had premed courses together and got along well.

I took the military seriously and was named Army cadet of the year as a sophomore. My junior year I was a member of the elite Sword Drill, competing for a place with other top-ranking members of my class. Yet three years at The Citadel was enough. I applied for early admission to medical school and was accepted. It was highly unusual to get this far and not "enjoy" the benefits of the senior year—so much so that when I declined an army officer's commission, I had to appear before the assistant commandant of cadets to explain my decision.

Volk and I had kept in touch. I phoned him. "Hey, Yank, my father is offering the use of his jeep this summer. My younger brother would go, too. You interested in going along, sharing costs?"

Volk accepted. We agreed to depart after his graduation.

Four days after my father's offer I called him back with a few questions. Was this still my trip? What if the jeep broke down? What if Ted and I didn't get along? With these issues settled, I talked with Ted. He understood that I could send him home or sell the jeep at any time I felt it necessary.

Ted was delighted to be included. He began getting my father's 1954 Willis jeep ready for the long trip. There was much to do, everything from checking out the rebuilt engine to getting together tools, spare parts, and tire-repair equipment. The jeep had removable doors and a canvas top covering the front seats. We extended the frame with plumbing pipe and made a plywood roof to carry our gear. We enclosed the back with canvas side and back curtains.

Meanwhile, I plunged into final exams. I liked the idea of phoning for my grades from out West. If I passed, fine. If I did poorly, I might not come back.

CHAPTER 2

On the Road

We left on the fourth of June. Although each of us had gathered our personal gear separately, "We all have hats the same shape, the same kind of packs with the same kind of dark glasses ... it looks pretty funny," Ted wrote in a letter home.

We set off at a modest thirty-five miles per hour, so as not to strain the jeep's small engine. At first this seemed frustratingly slow but after several days we wondered why everyone else was in such a hurry. We took turns driving three-hour shifts, usually covering a hundred miles each. At a shift change, the driver would move over to the front passenger seat and the back-seat person became the next driver, having been able to get a nap lying across the back seat. When the weather was good we took off the doors, stowed them on top, and rolled up the curtains.

It was a leisurely trip. Mostly we drove country roads but passed through the outskirts of Chicago where a "gas war" had brought the price down to twenty-four cents a gallon. We drove westward for endless miles surrounded by vast corn fields and were delighted to finally reach the open prairie where horned larks and western meadowlarks flew up from the roadside or sat on fence posts singing their melodies. We stopped at unexpected ponds to watch ducks and other waterfowl feed.

Our routine was simple. We camped by the side of the road when we got tired of driving. For breakfast we ate cereal and for lunch a sandwich. Supper was usually rice and beans. I took over as cook after we became ill eating Ted's grease-soaked pancakes. Under watchful eyes I divided the food, careful to give equal servings. We took turns with other chores. We got along well and talked little, content to watch the country change and enjoy a profound sense of freedom.

Usually we set up camp while there was still some daylight, but it was dark when we stopped outside Browning, Montana. We were thrilled the next morning to see the Rocky Mountains in the distance. We drove north through the grandeur of Glacier National Park and across the open Canadian prairie to Calgary, which was roughly halfway from South Carolina to Alaska. After another six hundred miles crossing monotonous farm lands, we arrived in Dawson Creek, British Columbia, the start of the fifteen-hundred-mile Alaska Highway to Delta Junction, Alaska, just one hundred miles short of Fairbanks.

The highway, also known as the Alcan, was built in 1942 by the U.S. Army to move military personnel and equipment to Alaska in response to the Japanese attack on the Aleutian Islands of Attu and Kiska. In 1961, it was still a dirt road, muddy when wet and dusty when dry. At our speed we were overtaken by everyone on the road, leaving us in a cloud of dust or covered with mud. When passed by a big truck, and there were many of them, we literally could not see the road until the dust settled.

It was a rough ride in the heavily loaded jeep, bumping along over the wash-boarded surface. For the first hour of a shift behind the wheel, whoever was driving dutifully tried to avoid the worst bumps and potholes, becoming less concerned about the rough ride the second hour and not caring at all the third. It was hard not to become irritated with the driver.

The constant jarring of the rough road caused our roof support pipes to break. We stopped several times to have them welded. They were a constant worry. The exhaust system would come apart periodically, too, leaving the muffler disconnected. We took turns crawling under the jeep to reconnect it and try to rig some way to keep it together.

Yet, our passage through this vast wilderness of forests, lakes, rivers, hills, and a horizon-to-horizon vista of mountains was rich compensation for any discomforts. This was what we had expected. I loved it.

We soaked off road grime at Liard Hot Springs, one-third of the way from Dawson Creek to the Alaska border. There and at other Canadian campgrounds in British Columbia and the Yukon Territory we met hardy tourists with whom we shared road stories and examined one another's broken windshields or headlights. A few times we met families who were headed to Alaska to homestead. I remember two young couples with several children, including a baby in arms, who had been poor dirt farmers in northern Florida. They sold all they had and together bought a truck, trailer, and small bulldozer. They were headed to

Alaska to find a new life. In their voices I heard hope and apprehension. I was awed.

It took us forty-eight hours of driving time on the Alcan to reach the Alaska border. About half of this was in one long, continuous round-the-clock push. We were surprised to get back onto pavement between the border and Fairbanks, a distance of about three hundred miles. The final stretch! We soon learned that pavement was not such a good thing. The wavy, frost-heaved road caused the jeep to sway in such a manner that the roof support pipes failed again. We stopped once more to have them welded.

On June 18, two weeks after leaving South Carolina, we finally arrived in the former gold-rush town of Fairbanks.

CHAPTER 3

Fairbanks, Alaska

Ted, Volk, and I were taking it easy in a Fairbanks campground, doing a little reading, when a news report on the radio drew our attention.

The newscaster reported that the day before a grizzly bear attacked a man in Haines who was in serious condition at the local hospital. He had parked his pickup, forded a small river, and walked several miles to a friend's homestead. On the return he was almost to the stream when a bear, unprovoked, rushed from nearby bushes.

"The man managed to shoot and kill the bear, but it fell across him, breaking both his legs," the newscaster reported. "He worked his way free of the bear and dragged himself across the stream to his truck. He drove to town using the rifle and a stick to work the pedals."

That settled it. We had been trying to decide whether to buy a large-caliber rifle. We had brought along a .22 Winchester for small animals and had no intent to hunt large ones. We drove into town and purchased a used, lever-action .30-.30 Winchester and a box of twenty cartridges for sixty-two dollars. The rifle was in good shape. A .30-.30 was considered to be minimal protection against a bear attack but we felt better anyway.

We looked up acquaintances of friends and invariably when the conversation drifted around to bears, we received much advice, such as:

"Don't run. It's usually a false charge."

"Shake a can with rocks in it, or tie it onto your pack. Then they won't bother you."

"Talk gently and back away. Don't run."

"Bears won't attack you unless with young or on a kill."

"Sometimes bears are unpredictable. Usually they will go their own way if not crowded."

We went to the post office to check general delivery. There was no mail from Bill Bennett, who had been waiting for grades. In an earlier letter he informed us that he was leaving South Carolina headed for Alaska by way of Seattle to visit his brother. The next day was June 21, Bill's deadline for meeting us in Fairbanks.

"If there's no note in the morning mail, we'll leave a letter for Bill and head for Circle," I said, making a decision for the three of us.

The next day we drove north on the Steese Highway where once again heavy road dust floated in and around the jeep, coating everything. Long sloping hills covered with spruce and birch gave way to treeless tundra as we crossed the higher elevations before descending into the Yukon Flats and on to the town of Circle on the Yukon River. Tourists in truck campers and trailers were scattered along the river, having driven to the northern end of the Alaska road system on the summer solstice to see the midnight sun.

We studied the rapid, heavily silted current of the Yukon before going to Frank Warren's general store where we ordered coffee and pie and listened to the talk for several hours. We needed a ride across the river so we could walk to Fort Yukon, but I was in no hurry. I came from a small town where it was better for a stranger to listen awhile before making a request. Volk's northeastern urban background differed. I could feel his impatience.

Cliff Fairchild, a bush pilot, came in with several tourists whom he had flown over to Fort Yukon so that they could cross the Arctic Circle.

Eventually I asked, "Mister Warren, you reckon there's anyone could take us across the river?"

"What do you want to go over there for?" he asked, leaning forward over the counter. "What are you boys up to?"

"We want to walk to Fort Yukon." I dared not say we intended to go much farther.

"Hey!" Mister Warren shouted to everyone within hearing distance. "These guys want to walk to Fort Yukon!"

Laughter erupted and three or four locals gathered around to question us, broad grins on their faces.

"The Flats are all water and willow!" one man said. "Nobody walks there, especially in the summer."

When the men learned we wanted to explore the remote region north of the Yukon for six to eight weeks, traveling on foot and depending on fish and rabbits for food, their reaction was unanimous: We would have to fly in.

"How much will that cost?"

With his finger, Cliff drew a circle on a large map of Alaska on the wall. "I'll take you that far in any direction for sixty dollars."

We studied the map. "Venetie, then," I said. We learned that it was an Indian village of about one hundred fifty people on the edge of the foothills of the Brooks Range about forty miles north of Fort Yukon.

"I'll pick you up in the morning."

"Park your jeep next to the store and I'll keep an eye on it," Frank Warren said.

The next morning, we were packed and waiting at the airstrip on the edge of town. Around noon a single-engine Piper Comanche landed downwind. This caught my attention since takeoffs and landings are usually made into wind.

The pilot stepped out. "Jules Thibedeau," he announced. "Cliff sent me. He's my partner. You want to go to Venetie? I'll treat you to pie and coffee at the store."

Jules was in his mid-thirties, open, pleasant and cheerful. We bought three candy bars each for our trip. We'd refrained from buying pop and candy on the way to Alaska. All three of us had lost weight.

We loaded our gear into the plane and were soon over the Yukon River. We had seen only one channel of the river at Circle but from the air saw many channels and hundreds of islands up and down the river. Toward the south we could see the White Mountains. Spread out below and in all other directions were the vast Yukon Flats. Sunlight glistened on water standing among expanses of green grass, willows, and alders with an occasional island of dark spruce. Small streams fed into the river, creating whorls and curls of clear water quickly swallowed by the muddy Yukon.

We flew over a long gravel airstrip, three radar towers, and scattered cabins. "Fort Yukon," Jules announced over the roar of the engine. "That's the Porcupine River, flows out of the Yukon Territory in Canada. Over there is the Chandalar."

Scattered rainstorms surrounded us as the foothills of the Brooks Range appeared on the horizon. "There's Venetie," Jules pointed toward some twenty cabins in the distance beside the Chandalar River. We circled around and lined up with a narrow dirt strip, barely the width of the plane.

Jules leaned toward me with some advice. "Don't just go off when you get there. Stay around. Ask about trails. Let people know what you want to do."

Our map showed that Venetie was on an Indian reservation. My plan was to land, apologize for our intrusion, and hike upriver along the Chandalar. The next settlement on the map above Venetie was Caro, but we hoped to go as far as Wiseman and then fly out.

To my surprise, what appeared to be the entire population of Venetie met us on the airstrip. We introduced ourselves to everyone, one by one. Chief Abraham Christian asked us to come to his log cabin to "sign in." Our packs and rifles quickly disappeared in the small crowd. I was apprehensive at first but we found our gear in a neat row against Abraham's log cabin.

As he made coffee on a Coleman stove, the chief asked "Where you go?"

"Caro," I answered.

"How come?"

"To buy more food so we can go on to Chandalar."

Abraham was quiet a moment, then said, "Nobody live there for long time, maybe ... 1913, 1914." Obviously we needed guidance.

"Better for you go up to Gold Camp on East Fork, see Johnny Frank. She wife, Sarah, too." He paused. "Johnny Frank know lots good story. Sure, you go there. Half way, good trail. Other part, little okay."

Sunlight streamed through the open door of the chief's cabin. I watched the floor and sipped coffee. The topographical maps we had were for the area of Caro, Chandalar, and Wiseman. I had cut out sections of the maps and taped them into sort of a scroll. The East Fork was not included.

"How far?" I asked.

Abraham studied the floor. "One night, maybe two. After Gold Camp, go Ackerman Lake. Big fish there—trout, jack fish, too."

Conversation was difficult. His English and my southern dialect were very different. Initially we were confused by the practice, common among the elderly, of using the wrong gender for pronouns. Later we learned that in Gwich'in, their native language, there was one pronoun for he, she, or it. Gender was determined by context. Chief Abraham's wife Annie entered, smiling shyly as Abraham introduced us. Their daughters, Barbara and Caroline, giggled and hid in the folds of Annie's dress. A son, Jim, came in.

"Our other son, John, in Anchorage hospital for TB," Abraham told us.

"You eat here?" Annie asked.

"Yes, thank you."

Abraham spoke to his son in Gwich'in. Jim left.

Abraham proudly showed us his garden. "Potatoes," he nodded toward a patch of some seventy-five healthy plants in neat rows, already three inches high. "I start them inside in cans, later move them outside."

We ducked to re-enter the cabin and heartily ate soup made of potatoes, onions, and dried duck meat. Future meals were uncertain. The rice, beans, and other food in our packs would not last long unless supplemented by what we could hunt or fish. As we drank tea, Jim returned with Stanley Frank, a grandson of Johnny and Sarah Frank. He had just returned to Venetie after six months of Army training in California. He was going to walk up to the East Fork of the Chandalar to visit his grandparents and offered to show us the way. We gladly accepted.

"Maybe we leave tomorrow."

"How far?"

"Maybe one day."

"How many miles?"

"Gee, I don't know." Long pause. "Maybe thirty-two, thirty-six miles."

"You can stay in my father-in-law's cabin. Ginnis is downriver at fish camp," Abraham offered.

The chief led us to a small log cabin on the other-side of his potato patch. He pushed open the door. "You go in."

I stooped to enter the nearly barren room, neatly kept. Soon it was cluttered with our gear. I sat on my blanket-roll. Volk and I lighted our pipes. As I smoked I marveled at our warm reception by the villagers. The little I had read about the Gwich'in led me to expect a strained, uncomfortable encounter. We were not only accepted but also made to feel truly welcome and graciously cared for.

After awakening early the next morning, we soon had an audience of children outside. They crowded around the single window and open door, competing for a look at these strangers. One of the oldest, a boy about twelve, introduced himself as Isaac Sam. We invited him in.

We shook hands as we spoke our names.

"Coffee?" I soon regretted the offer. Isaac had not seen instant coffee before and put two heaping spoonfuls of our meager supply into a small cup. He bravely downed the potent result with an extra-generous helping of sugar.

As we packed our gear, Isaac watched awhile before asking, "Where you going?"

"Going to Gold Camp with Stanley."

"Stanley went fishing upriver this morning."

Apparently we would not be leaving that day as planned. The next morning when we tracked down Stanley, he told us, "Maybe rain today."

I told Abraham we wanted to help get food. The chief asked David Henry to allow us to accompany him fishing that evening. We followed David several miles upriver through a spruce forest to a slough off the Chandalar.

"I show you Indian way to catch grayling." David took out a small section of line with a hook, which he attached to a long, dry willow pole that he cut. A small piece of willow leaf, whitish on one side, served as the initial lure. He quietly snuck up to where we could see fish in the clear water. Hiding behind a bush, David gently jiggled the hook near the fish. After his first catch, a sliver of the flesh and skin from the grayling's throat made good bait.

ISSAC SAM CAME to the small cabin to visit each morning. On the third day as he prepared a cup of coffee, he announced, "Stanley leave already."

"What! Where to?"

"Gold Camp. He says come now."

We scrambled to ready our packs. Hurriedly we thanked Abraham and Annie Christian for their hospitality. The chief asked for our names and addresses, explaining, "One time somebody come up here and go out. Never tell she name. Never come back. We can't even tell the state trooper who that is."

Isaac led us to the trail. Out of breath, confused, and unhappy about our erratic start, we struggled to catch up with Stanley. We followed him a considerable distance before he acknowledged our presence with a nod.

The trail was dry for the three miles to Big Lake. Then we waded in knee-deep water for a mile or more around the west side of the lake. On the far shore the trail climbed a slope into the foothills, leaving the broad Yukon Flats. Water ran ankle-deep in the depressions of the trail. Our feet remained soaked. We met three hunters and a pack dog coming down the mountainside. They'd had no luck in three days of hunting.

Volk began to get blisters and fell behind. Several times we stopped to wait. I was glad for the breaks. We arrived at a beautiful little lake on the mountainside. We'd walked only nine miles in six hours.

"Cranberry Lake," Stanley said. "We call it *Natl'at Van*. We could camp here."

Our packs came off in an instant, and we started a fire to dry socks and feet. Our knoll was on dry ground in spruce and birch with a good view of the lake where grebes, gulls, and several species of ducks searched for food. A large lynx emerged from the woods and crept into the lakeside grass. We watched enthralled for half an hour as he moved stealthily back and forth in a low crouch. The ducks saw him, too. When the lynx crossed our trail at the head of the lake, he stood up, stretched, and disappeared into the woods.

In late June the sun didn't set but when it passed behind the mountain, it turned uncomfortably cold. We had left insulated underwear at Abraham and Annie's, a decision we would regret many times. I thought a blanket and poncho would be sufficient since there would be no darkness for several months. However, condensation collected inside the poncho and soaked the blanket. Fortunately Volk had a decent sleeping bag. Ted and I slept fitfully until the sun rose high enough to warm us. Later we rearranged our activities to hike during the cooler hours and sleep when the sun struck.

The next morning Stanley was up and had started a fire. We fixed soup and coffee and shared Stanley's canned corned beef and cold pancakes. He had packed a sleeping bag, a bit of food, tea, a pot, a few personal articles, and an old .22 Special.

"My father Nathaniel used it to kill caribou, moose, wolf, and even brown bear. He shoot bear five times, all in heart," Stanley said.

The trail angled upward across a mountain. Stanley moved at a fast pace, and I was determined to keep up. We had set out from Venetie with full canteens, but had not refilled them as water ran in the trail. Several times I stooped to fill my canteen.

"Not yet," Stanley said.

We stopped where the trail crossed just above a little cut bank. Below, clear water flowed over a small mud flat.

"Here you get water." Relieved of my pack, I stretched, picked up my canteen and cup, and stepped down to the stream.

"Watch out for mud," Stanley warned.

I stepped onto clumps of grass but could not reach water deep enough to scoop so I took another step onto the mud. Immediately I began to sink and had to step forward to keep my balance. Now both legs were sinking. I fell forward across a clump of grass but could not pull out my legs, by then buried in mud above my knees. I grasped a little tree. Stanley and Ted had to pull me out.

"Sometime moose get stuck here. Die, too. Even bear scared of it."

My adrenaline was running high. I was angry that I'd not had a better warning, but I was learning to pay more attention to Gwich'in instructions, which were frequently minimal or non-verbal. Nothing further was said. We started a fire and fixed coffee. I wondered why Stanley had suggested I refill my canteen in this dangerous spot.

My anger gave way to a feeling of awe as we looked out over the flats, Big Lake close below, and across the vast undisturbed country south toward Fort Yukon. This was why I'd come, to find a place beyond roads and development.

In the afternoon Ted began to fall behind. Stanley seemed never to grow weary, but graciously stopped when we needed a break. Across the shoulder of the mountain the trail became dry as we descended to a spot between two small lakes.

"Maybe we camp here. Sometimes moose come in morning," Stanley said.

I dropped my pack. That day we'd walked only another nine miles. Ted and Volk had large heel blisters and I had one on the ball of my left foot. The second night Ted and I slept fitfully again due to the cold. The sun was obscured. It began to rain. Once during the night I awoke with a numb foot that had slipped out of the poncho. It took an hour of rubbing to restore feeling.

In the morning Stanley had a fire ready again. Coffee, a package of soup, and the last of the pancakes made our breakfast. We packed and started up what Stanley called Rock Mountain. The steep trail was overhung with wet willow and alder. A light rain fell. As usual Stanley kept a fast pace, softly whistling while using a stick to knock water off the brush ahead. Near the top, no longer able keep up, I stopped to rest standing up. From the summit Stanley pointed out Bush Mountain, Martin Mountain, and several other peaks. All had names in Gwich'in and English. Wilderness spread in all directions. Behind us were the

Yukon Flats. Ahead were waves of foothills and smaller mountains rolling northward to the majestic Brooks Range. We were above the tree line. Except for a rocky area with patches of lichen on top, the rest of Rock Mountain was brushy. We pushed through knee- and thigh-high brush for several miles along the ridge.

Stanley stopped and pointed, "Down there. That's Gold Camp and the East Fork." It took me a few minutes to see the small cabin and a wall tent barely visible beyond the river. No other human disturbance was visible anywhere in the entire valley. Below the cabin, a creek entered the river. Downriver a massive mountain rose up, its peak hidden by dark clouds. We reached the river that afternoon on painfully blistered feet. Ted's were the worst but he did not complain. We were tired but beginning to toughen.

"Make fire here," Stanley told us.

Thick smoke rose from green spruce boughs we heaped on the fire at Stanley's direction. He shot his .22 rifle several times but it made little noise. He asked me to shoot the .30-.30. I did so, once.

For a while we watched expectantly. Then Volk and Ted broke out fishing rods. I dozed in the afternoon sun on the bank of the East Fork of the Chandalar River, now fifty or sixty miles above the Arctic Circle. Ted and Volk were looking intently upriver when I awoke.

"Johnny Frank coming," Stanley announced.

Across the swift main channel, a small man stood in a little green canoe. He wore an old tweed coat, shirt, and tie. He paddled into the current and was propelled rapidly downstream, balancing as he ferried toward our bank. He swept past us, intently watching the water, a pipe clenched in his teeth, his dark face shaded by an old-style peaked Stetson hat. We rushed down to the river and caught the boat as it came to shore. A smile broke across the man's face as he stepped onto the bank.

We pulled the boat back upriver. Two at a time he took us across to an island. Volk and I were last. The man took my pack and rifle and carefully balanced them in the boat, a light wooden frame covered with canvas and sealed with paint.

He pointed me into the bow and nosed the canoe into the current. There was little freeboard. I balanced myself. "Where you go?" he asked.

"Ackerman Lake."

He looked me over, smiled, and held out his hand. "Good. I go with you."

"Good!" I laughed, taking his hand. "I don't know the way!"

I had only vague directions from Chief Abraham Christian to get from Gold Camp to Ackerman Lake. We had no maps of this area.

"I saw you smoke before I hear rifle. By golly, long time nobody come. No canoe, too. Leave it down at the creek." So he had gone to get the canoe, changed into his fancy clothes and come over. "Cuff link, too!" He gave an almost silent laugh.

I turned slightly to look at his wrist, his arm extended between paddle strokes. The large flat hat brim shadowed a wrinkled, dark, jovial face. Quick eyes watched the river, darting to me.

"What you name?"

"Mike Holloway."

He nodded, "Johnny Frank."

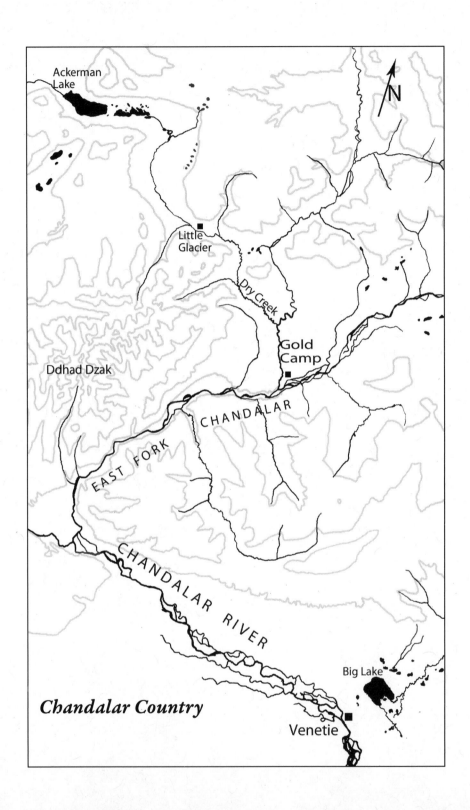

Ackerman
Lake

N

Little
Glacier

Dry Creek

Gold
Camp

Ddhad Dzak

CHANDALAR

EAST FORK

CHANDALAR RIVER

Big Lake

Chandalar Country

Venetie

CHAPTER 4

Gold Camp

Shallow creeks separated small gravel islands. We carried the boat across the island, using it again to cross the last channel. An elderly woman shuffled from the canvas wall tent. A little boy ran down the bank to meet us at the water's edge. Four or five large dogs on short chains rose, stretched, and stared at us.

We were introduced to Johnny's wife, Sarah, who held and patted our hands. "Hello, hello," she smiled. "You drink tea?" motioning to a pot on the oil drum stove outside the tent.

"Thank you."

She directed us into the tent. Buhach powder burned in the doorway to discourage mosquitoes. Pilot bread, butter, and jam were set out.

"How long you live here?" I asked.

"Long time—1934," Johnny answered. Sarah spoke little English. "You see those old cabins on the other side, near little creek? First time, live there. Nathaniel, my son, live there too. That Stanley's father. Stanley born there."

Johnny was small, maybe five-foot-two, and looked as if he weighed about one hundred pounds. He was eighty-one but looked half that age. A lean man, he moved easily. His skin was the color of burnished copper with few wrinkles, except for smile creases around his mouth and eyes. His face was triangular with high, prominent cheekbones accentuated by sunken cheeks below. His gaze was direct without being threatening. His brown eyes were ringed by a narrow band of silver, creating a startling effect. He was missing several teeth.

Sarah was a couple of inches shorter than Johnny. She moved about carefully with a slow, shuffling walk. She wore a long skirt that touched the ground and a cardigan sweater over a cotton shirt. A scarf framed her oval face exposing iron-gray hair above a lightly wrinkled forehead. Her dark eyes were almond shaped with slightly hooded upper lids.

We made ourselves comfortable as Johnny began to talk. Previously he and Sarah had lived farther north near Arctic Village. Johnny had prospected at Gold Camp many years before.

"Lots of color here," he said. "Good place for moose, too, so we move here."

He and his son Nathaniel once dug a deep hole at the first old home-site, prospecting for gold. The work took months, thawing permafrost with wood fires, foot-by-foot, and digging and hauling dirt out by bucket. They took turns, one working in the hole, and the other up on top.

They were joined by Moses Cruikshank and a white man named Ambo. Johnny started a cabin for them, which they finished. They sunk two or three holes using their boiler to thaw the ground. Periodically the pan washings showed "lots of color" but they made no strike. One day the hole collapsed while they were drinking tea above ground. That was the end of gold mining for Johnny.

"That okay," he said. "No use for money anyway."

We chatted awhile, then Johnny and Sarah spoke with their grandson Stanley in Gwich'in. Sarah prepared pancakes and boiled moose meat previously cut into strips and sun-dried. We gorged ourselves, drank more tea, and sleepily sank into a foot-deep covering of soft willow boughs covering the tent floor. Soon it became difficult to concentrate enough to understand Johnny's stories.

"You play checker?" Out came a checkerboard. I learned there was more to this game than I'd thought. Johnny easily beat each of us, laughing and hardly looking at the board. "Used to be, long time ago, everybody play checker at Fort Yukon. Well, by and by, nobody beat me!"

Johnny ushered us to the small log cabin nearby. It was about ten by fourteen feet. "You stay here. Sleep good." He brought extra blankets. We tossed for the single bed, made of small poles. Ted won. We snuggled into the blankets, falling asleep almost immediately.

The next morning we could hardly move after a big breakfast of oatmeal, dry meat, pancakes with syrup, and coffee and tea. Stanley went fishing and returned in a few hours with grayling. This spurred us to want to provide food for the camp, too, so we went fishing. Ted and Volk had difficulty using their spinning and fly rods within the confines of the small creek. I did better fishing Indian style, as we had learned from David Henry in Venetie.

Around the evening meal of grayling, Johnny told stories about their lives, Eskimo-Indian powers, wars, and old times. It was difficult for us to follow his stories. His English was broken and we spoke no Gwich'in. Yet his stories were riveting.

"Used to be I'm medicine man. Give it up. Read Bible. I read Bible four times. Never go to school, too." He laughed his almost-silent chuckle, his body shaking, his face wrinkled in mirth.

I wanted to hear more about medicine men but he spoke of the Bible. For forty years he carried the Bible on his trap line, working laboriously over the difficult words alone in his tent.

"Fur good price that time," Johnny said. "Lots of white men, even missionary don't know Bible. I know. I ask them questions. They can't say nothing.

"First time I kill moose—maybe eighteen year old that time. Borrow rifle, .44 Winchester. First time I see white man, too, that year."

"You ever kill moose with bow and arrow?" I asked him.

"No. Lots of people, sure. Not me. Just rifle."

The next few days we interspersed eating with work around the camp. Johnny had begun to build a second cabin at their winter site, about two hundred yards below the tent. It was a few logs high and would be more spacious, about twenty by twenty-four feet. Johnny chose the trees to be made into logs. He pointed to one with a twisted, spiral grain and laughed, "No good that one—*Vasaagihdzak*. Good story. Tonight I tell you."

We cut, dragged, and peeled logs. Johnny fit the logs and cut the notches. Lawrence, his seven-year-old grandson, gathered sphagnum moss for chinking between the logs. The walls went up rapidly with breaks for pipe-smoking and storytelling.

"Last winter I hunt caribou," Johnny pointed to the hills opposite us. "I forget to set that sled brake. When I shoot, dogs run fast. Lucky, I catch that sled. Maybe lose dogs, see?"

After catching the sled with one hand, the dogs dragged him several miles before stopping. By then his arm was paralyzed.

"My arm no good," Johnny said. "Only move a little my hand—not strong, too. Just old lady, Lawrence, and me. Not much good to hunt. Lucky we got caribou meat. Set snare for rabbit, too."

The stretched nerves took more than three months to recover. Until then, Johnny whipsawed floorboards for the new cabin with one arm, managing a large saw on scaffolding built out from the bank.

Usually whipsawing boards required two men working together. It was a tough job. The man on the lower end of the long handsaw stood in a pit. Sawdust continually fell in his face. Worse yet, mosquitoes collected in the pit, out of the breeze.

That evening Sarah cooked a large supper of boiled moose made from dried meat, rice, dumplings, tea, and bannock bread. She made the bread in a frying pan from flour, baking soda, and water.

After dinner, Johnny sat back and filled his pipe. "Remember I tell you today about *Vasaagihdzak*," Johnny laughed. "Lots of old stories about him. He travel all over. All time cause trouble. Play tricks, see?

"Well, one time he kill moose with arrow. *Vasaagihdzak* start to skin moose. Well, every kind animal come around. They all hungry, see? That time everybody speak same language—people, animals too.

"Well, they say, '*Vasaagihdzak*, we got no food. We hungry. Give us meat.'

"'No,' he say.

"'My partner, we hungry. Give us meat.'

"*Vasaagihdzak* just play with meat, say nothing," Johnny chuckled, removing his pipe to talk.

"'Grandpa, share meat. You got plenty. We got nothing.'

"'No.'

"*Vasaagihdzak* just tease them." Johnny chuckled, cleared his throat, coughed, and spit into a can. Sarah sat on the bed, leaning forward with her eyes closed, listening, now and then nodding and laughing. She seemed to be concentrating to understand English.

"Well, *Vasaagihdzak* eat lots. By golly, want to eat more but can't do it. Too full, see? He go between two big spruce tree. He magic, *Vasaagihdzak*. Want tree to squeeze him. Clean out gut. Make him shit, so can eat more moose. Tell tree, 'Squeeze me.'

"They squeeze but don't let go. Just hold him. Stuck, see?" Johnny laughed. Sarah smiled.

"Animals eat all that moose. Crow, camp robber, bear, wolf, everybody clean it up.

"*Vasaagihdzak* can't do nothing. Get mad, too. When just bones left trees let go. He grab tree and twist it, hard too. Make it twisted. Today, you remember, I tell you '*Vasaagihdzak* make that tree twisted'?

"Good story, huh?" Johnny laughs and Sarah chuckles.

"Well, just bones left. She break bones, make grease. Hungry. Stomach empty now, see? Put grease in bag and take to lake. Want to make it cold. He tell muskrat, 'Tie bag on tail and swim. Don't break it.'

"Muskrat say, 'Okay, but don't scare me.'

"*Vasaagihdzak* want to know what will happen so he throw a little piece of moss. Scare muskrat. Muskrat dive, break bag. Grease go out, all over lake. Sometime you see that little scum on top lake? *Vasaagihdzak*!" We all laughed. Johnny puffed his pipe, silent for a few minutes. "Well, lots *Vasaagihdzak* story. All kinds story. *Ch'iteehaakwaii*, crow, too. Well, go sleep now. Use little cabin."

We flipped coins. Ted won the bed again and a game of cribbage. We slept warmly.

AFTER SEVERAL NIGHTS, I expressed my concern to Johnny that the three of us were eating too much of his and Sarah's food, that maybe it was time for us to move on to Ackerman Lake. Johnny knocked ashes from his pipe and looked me in the eye. "You stay one month, okay. Two month, okay. You stay three month, maybe talk about pay."

I could hardly believe such generosity. Johnny explained that he was waiting for a "grub" delivery by small plane from Fort Yukon. After it came, he would leave for Ackerman Lake with us.

During the days we fished, worked on the new cabin, or went upriver to cut trees for firewood. We hauled the logs to the river and floated them to Gold Camp as a raft. Stanley might return to Venetie and we wanted to leave Sarah and Lawrence a good wood supply. In the mornings Stanley took Ted out to set and check rabbit snares. They became friends, though four or five years different in age.

Sarah was kind, smiling, touching our shoulders and calling us grandson in Gwich'in, which she tried to help us learn. Although only seven, Lawrence cheerfully did chores, had his own snares, and handled a .22 rifle or ax with skill and care.

One morning at breakfast we heard an engine. Everyone became silent. The sound seemed out of place. Johnny broke the silence, smiling. "Maybe Thanksgiving today!"

A yellow, single-engine aircraft approached over the mountains, buzzed the camp, and banked around sharply to line up with a landing strip cleared of willows on a gravel bar opposite the camp. Sand and pebbles flew as the wheels touched down with a bump. The plane bounced into the air for a second before settling down. We took the larger canoe over to the sandbar.

The Wien Air Alaska pilot, Keith Harrington, climbed out of the Cessna 185. As he shook hands all around, he said, "Johnny, you've got to fix that landing strip!"

We helped Keith unload six hundred fifty pounds of "grub"—rice, flour, sugar, coffee, tea, tobacco, apples, oranges, a crate of eggs, dried fruit, mush, onions, pilot bread, and candy. We ferried everything back to camp and stored it in the cache, a flat covered platform built on four-foot stilts made from logs to keep scavenging animals out of the food supplies. Pieces of flattened metal from five-gallon Blazo fuel cans were fashioned into barriers at the base of each leg to discourage small animals.

Keith came for tea and a chat. A six-footer, he towered over Johnny and Sarah. They exchanged news and gossip. Then he flew away, leaving Gold Camp once more quiet and isolated.

In the afternoon I sawed wood. The others filled dips in the landing strip. Then Ted, Volk, and I went into the river for a bath, encouraged by Stanley, who had gone swimming the previous day. The water was icy cold. We bathed standing in the shallows and washed our clothes quickly while the mosquitoes were temporarily absent. We had no change of pants or shirts.

That evening Sarah fixed an extra-large meal, including a bowl of cooked apples. We lay back on the fragrant bed of freshly cut spruce boughs. After the large meals we became lethargic and had to force ourselves to haul water or wood, or go fishing, but this time Johnny passed out cigarettes and we settled back. Usually a story followed.

CHAPTER 5

Bear Camp

"We go Ackerman Lake today," Johnny announced over breakfast. "We take two pack dogs, Blackie and Diamond. Leader, Granger and *Vat'aii* stay here."

The huskies sensed a trip and watched alertly as we sorted gear. As Stanley and Lawrence walked among them, they began jumping up, barking, and begging to go. Once their packs were secured, Diamond and Blackie paraded by the other dogs, who barked and lunged at them, stretching their chains to the limit. The dogs packed about twenty-five pounds each, leaving Johnny with a pleasant fifteen pounds.

Johnny led, often stopping to point out tracks or signs, light his pipe, explain things, or tell a story. He walked slowly but steadily and covered ground well. We walked single file: Johnny first, then me, Ted and last Volk. We had gone a mile when Johnny turned, "By golly, I forget mosquito head net."

I understood this indirect request and went back for it. Sarah was glad to see me, as he'd also forgotten his coat. On my return, he only commented, "Good."

Johnny stopped to refill his pipe, nodding toward a flock of small birds on some branches near us. "What you call that one?"

"Chickadee, chickadee," I answered.

Johnny laughed and repeated the sound, so like the bird's own.

"Chandalar people say *ch'idzigyaak.*"

"Old story." Johnny's eyes twinkled. His look was direct but not harsh. The curved Peterson pipe hung from his teeth. I waited. Ted stopped beside me.

Johnny tapped lightly with his fingertips against the opposite hand. "What you call that bird?"

"Woodpecker."

"Well, winter time, not much grub. Cold, too, maybe fifty below. When other birds leave, chickadee stay here.

"Chickadee tell woodpecker, 'My partner, this winter you stay here. No trouble. Lots of food. No use to fly long way south this winter.' Finally, woodpecker says, 'Okay.'

"By and by getting more cold, every day. No food, too. Woodpecker can't make it. 'My partner,' he ask chickadee, 'when we get food?'

"'No worry, pretty soon now.'

"Well, by and by woodpecker starve.

"Chickadee says 'Now, my partner, lots of food.'—"Johnny's body shook in laughter. "Those old people say chickadee trick all kinds of birds and make stay too long. He eat them."

We walked along the creek behind Gold Camp, crossing gravel bars and passing among spruce and birch through deep moss. The ground was flat. Hills rose against the skyline as we walked toward them and those behind us, across the East Fork, retreated gradually. Occasionally the trail passed close to pools of clear water where grayling gathered away from the fast current. Finally we arrived at a crossing. Johnny sat on a log and removed his boots. The upper part was made of caribou leg skin with the hair still attached. The foot was tanned moose skin, over which he wore rubber slippers.

Johnny waded into the water using a pole for balance. We removed our boots and the dogs' packs and waded in. The initial shock was penetrating. The cold water came to mid-thigh. The strong current and shifting rocks brought a rush of adrenaline and focused our attention on getting across safely.

An hour later Johnny turned, "Sometime wolf hole here. We go check." He pointed his rifle into the woods. "You make tea," he instructed Ted and Volk. "Keep dogs here." A quarter-mile in was a cut-bank left from old streambed.

"By golly, fresh wolf tracks!" We had seen many old tracks on the gravel bars after crossing the creek. Now we had found a den opening in the bank.

"Look! Pup tracks. Fresh shit, too," Johnny exclaimed. Moss and scattered spruce covered the ground above the entrance.

"Stop up holes," he explained as he pushed a bundle of sticks firmly into the entrance. We located a dozen smaller openings and closed those, too. A depression in the moss over an opening indicated where the parents often lay guarding their litter. Johnny pushed a long pole through the entrance to locate the main chamber. Once we had found it, we removed moss and ground cover and dug into the den from above. The chamber was about four by six feet with tunnels leading away from it. Johnny set a steel trap in the center and we remade the roof with small poles and moss.

At another den nearby we repeated the process. In 1961, the bounty on wolves was sixty dollars, no matter the size or age. After rejoining Ted, Volk, and the dogs, we all had tea and dry meat and then walked another mile to where a small stream entered the creek.

"We camp here. Six Mile Fork," Johnny announced. "Good place for grayling and rabbit."

We gathered wood and water. Johnny retrieved a homemade tin stove and stovepipe that he'd hidden in a tree. Ted and Volk fished. Johnny showed me how to set snares on rabbit trails that crossed a nearby thicket. In a narrow place where the trail passed between small trees, he jammed a stout stick diagonally across the narrow opening low enough to make a rabbit duck down to get under it. To this he attached a noose made of braided picture-hanging wire. The noose was two and a half to three inches in diameter. Finally he carefully set twigs and dry grass stalks to guide the rabbit to the center of the loop. When the rabbit ducked, its ears would go back along the body as its nose entered the loop. The braided wire would tighten and choke the rabbit.

Later, Johnny drank tea and had a smoke but would not wait for the grayling to finish boiling. "I go back and get Stanley, ax, and shovel," he said, having mentioned several times that we needed these tools but getting no volunteers to go back to camp for them.

"Tonight?" I asked, ready to eat and sleep.

"Sure. Come back tomorrow. Give me you poncho. You use my blankets."

I guiltily watched him go downstream, slow and steady, with his rifle over his shoulder, the poncho in a burlap sack on his back. At eighty-one, Johnny had incredible stamina.

Ted won our nightly cribbage game. We slept warmly with the extra blankets.

AT MID-DAY, we met Johnny and Stanley at the wolf dens. We opened one den to check the trap, pushing a pole out the side tunnels to mark their direction, and then dug in from outside. After examining nine or ten holes Johnny noticed that we had blocked out the pups. They had tried to dig in around our blockages.

At the second den, the pups had gotten in, so we blocked the tunnels again and dug into the central chamber. There we found a pup caught in our trap. She was beautiful, the size of a cocker spaniel. She was friendly when we released her foot and never tried to bite. After holding her for a while I asked, "Johnny, may I keep her? I'll pay the bounty."

"No. Danger, when grow up."

I turned my head, unable to watch. Stanley clubbed and skinned her, leaving in the front leg bones. To collect the state bounty, it was necessary to leave on the left leg only. As this was easy to confuse, it was better to leave both. We worked several more hours and caught a second cub, this one wedged in a side tunnel for which he'd grown too large.

Around the fire that evening Johnny told stories about wolves as we ate rabbit soup and drank tea.

"One time Indian raise wolf for dog team. Just wolf. No dog. I think maybe six. Well, okay for long time. No trouble. Strong. Smart, too. Then one time, maybe no food—something—out hunting and they kill that man. They eat him, too, little bit. Somebody find him."

Johnny said wolves killed many caribou and moose. He had seen two wolves kill a Dall sheep once. He felt they killed mostly for food. I asked him if he thought wolves were bad.

"No, not bad. Just like dog. But sometimes lots wolf is hungry. See anything, just kill and eat up. Hungry, that's all. Wolf kill moose easy."

"How many wolves?"

"Just one ... sometimes three. One time old lady got sled, dogs. She was breaking trail on snowshoes. Tent, stove, everything in sled. On top of mountain were two little high places with no trees, just willow, maybe that high." Johnny held his hand knee-high. "No timber so I can see long way. Well, I see three wolves and one young bull moose, two-year-old, strong. Moose go fast in soft snow; everybody know that. That bull go fast, take big steps. That time I go fast, too. I run on big trail snowshoes, follow track.

"Those wolves kill moose. Not five minutes! Those big teeth catch here," he grabbed his throat, "Squeeze tight. Cut like knife. In half-hour they eat half that big bull. No timber, I can see good. Then those three big wolves go up mountain ... fat, moving slow.

"I never kill wolf that time. Funny ... you know medicine? Used to be I had strong medicine. I dream wolf. Never kill for long time. Even if wolf come close, like that," he pointed to a spot four or five feet away. "I can't hit him. I shoot ... but nothing." Johnny sat back and smoked awhile in silence.

"Wolf knows my dog and never bothers, even (if) my dogs chase caribou. That's when wolf usually kill dog. One time I got good leader, but something wrong with both sides of head, around ears. Well, I don't like to kill dog, but pretty bad. I'm scared I won't kill dog first shot, see? I'm good shooter then; seven years I never miss. She look back at me last time. I shoot, hit her in side. She jump and I shoot again. Knock her down. Never get up. That night, everywhere—two miles, five miles, maybe ten—wolf holler long time. They know I kill that dog."

"They want to eat that dog?"

"No! They know my dog, see? Never hurt my dogs. Well, I tell old lady, 'I go kill wolf.' I go up little creek one mile. Maybe fifteen, no ... seventeen wolf on this side—thirty over there. All stop holler."

"Were you scared?"

"No. I dream wolf, I tell you. She don't hurt man. Maybe if (there are) one hundred ... but they are hungry then. Well, wolves stop holler. I go around little hill. Go fast, too. Then I wait in little place. Wolf come around. Pretty soon three wolves come. I got rifle ready. I shot last one first, then next. Three wolf, I kill all three. After that I kill lots of wolves ... maybe ten that year. One thing, wolf skin worth nothing that time ... maybe one dollar. No bounty, too."

"Why did you shoot them?"

"I tell you, I see those three wolves eat half a moose, fast, too. Eat too much!" They were his competitors for food.

"Used to be one place other side of Heart Mountain. My son Hamel and I were hunting there. Hard ground on one side river. Animals travel good there, no tracks. We see big bull moose stand up and look around, shake his head this way, that way. Then seven moose stand up little way farther, like horses! I tell Hamel and he shoot two bulls. Fat, too, by golly! This thick the bacon," he held up three fingers.

"We made skin boat, scow. No sugar that time. Hamel smoked, too, Velvet tobacco, but he got no tobacco. I got leaf tobacco. We go downriver fast. See lots of moose on riverbank. Never stand up; just see head. Beaver, too. See big ones but we never bother."

"Why so many moose, maybe no wolves?" I asked.

"Lots of wolves there. I never see but lots of wolf shit. Ground too hard for tracks but lots of wolf shit. Lots of moose and wolves at that place. One place we see two wolf skulls, broken. One big bull or cow hit with back leg and knock wolf maybe twenty-five feet ... just dead wolf.

"Another time I was on top of big hill. No timber maybe three miles. Sixty-five below. We need meat. I see cow and calf ... ten wolves all around. They take calf first. I run hard, just sweat all over. My face just wet! I can't see good. I shoot but never hit.

"Wolf kill bear, too ... maybe she got family and don't want bear to bother. Bear come along. Big wolf and wife hide. Bear come by and big wolf jump, catch throat. At same time, wife catch prick, balls, too. Bear just make one noise, then can't say nothing. Can't fight, too. Die in maybe five minutes.

"Bear, too, my friend. Black bear is like dog. I dream bear, too; never hurt me. Four times I kill bear in hole. One time I see where bear go in with two cubs, maybe the day before. He cover entrance with light snow but I follow. I see frost from breath. Get rifle ready, .30-.30, loaded. Brush snow off with one hand. Bear look up, three feet away. I shoot one time right here," he touched his forehead. "I reach down and catch little one here (by the scruff of the neck), pull out and cut throat."

"The little one can't live by itself?"

"No, wolf find little bear that winter. Two times I see where wolf kill big bear in hole; no bones left, just hair. Bear never wake up.

"Long time ago when man find bear hole, he go get help. Three men come back. They got two long poles and one club, maybe five feet. Catch bear across neck … Other man hits bear in back of head, two times, kill easy.

"Well, too late. Go to bed now. Get sleep."

I awoke early the next morning, glad to hear Johnny starting a fire. He, too, had slept poorly. We drank coffee. "Just one cup coffee, I drink. Then just tea, tea, all day drink tea. That's my wine," he laughed. As we sipped slowly, he asked, "You friend, what she name?"

"Richard Volkwein. We call him Rick or Volk."

The old man slowly repeated Volk's name. He smoked and then asked, "You brother?"

"Ted," I said, realizing he'd not been using our names in the week we'd been together, I thought of Huck Finn trying to get someone to remind him of his forgotten alias. "My name is Mike."

He nodded.

I CHECKED SNARES and found two rabbits. Johnny caught a ground squirrel in a trap. He quickly skinned the rabbits, then stuck a stick through the ground squirrel and held it in the fire to burn off the fur. The skin blistered and the burnt fur stank. Johnny scraped the skin with a stick, then gutted it, cut it up, and threw it into a pot to boil. I learned that this preserved the fat between the skin and muscle, for which ground squirrels and porcupines are favored. Few of the local foods contain fat, which most Gwich'in crave.

THE DAY WAS warm with no breeze. Initially the trail was good but later crossed fields of tussocks. These were exasperating. No description is more accurate than in Robert Marshall's book about Wiseman, *Arctic Village*, written in the 1930s. At the time tussocks were referred to as "niggerheads." Marshall wrote:

> *A niggerhead, I suppose, among all the gifts of bountiful nature, ranks as the most cursed. It starts as a little clump of sedge, and over a long period of years gradually builds upward and outward into a great, mushroom shaped, sod-like mass. The end product is from two to four feet high, perhaps a foot thick at the base, and double that size on the top. So close together do these niggerheads grow that it is impossible to walk between them, while if you try to step over them you become exhausted in no time. So what you attempt is to balance upon their tottering tops as you walk along. This works splendidly if you happen to step on the very middle, but the niggerheads are so overbalanced that on the frequent occasions when you miss the center of gravity, over they flop, and down you go into the mud beneath. Occurring once this merely provokes profanity. Occurring fifty to one hundred times to a mile it is likewise exhausting.*

• • •

AS THE TUSSOCKS slowed us down, swarms of mosquitoes attacked us. I wore a thick wool shirt over a thin cotton one, the sleeves always buttoned, hands gloved, pants tied around the ankles, a kerchief about my neck. The swarm thickened about us. At rest stops we played a game—who could kill the most mosquitoes with one slap on the thigh. Ted led with eighteen. Mosquito repellent kept them a few inches away from the face. Their constant buzz and presence forced me to put on a head net. We each had one small bottle of repellent.

We lost the trail through a mile of tussocks and found it again as we crossed the bed of Dry Creek, or *Chekheckanjik' Chanjik*. After crossing another field of tussocks, Johnny, Ted, and I entered a small grove of spruce trees. Volk was about one hundred feet back. After each rest, the dogs tried to walk directly behind Johnny until persuaded to drop back. They were difficult to walk behind, always in the way. Now they were behind Volk.

Suddenly Volk yelled, "Look, a bear!" He sounded excited but there was no fear in his voice. I looked to the right, saw nothing, and turned to look to my left. Then Volk screamed, "It's charging, it's charging. What do I do?"

I caught a glimpse of movement in the trees. The large blond bear moved silently with tremendous speed—directly toward Richard. I brought the rifle to my shoulder but at first could not see the sights due to the head net. I waited for Johnny to shoot first. He had given me firm instructions: "We see moose, bear, I shoot first. You don't know." But Johnny's rifle was caught in the canvas case. As he struggled to remove it, Johnny made a long, loud high-pitched sound. The bear immediately turned and then charged the pack dogs. Johnny and I both fired and the bear rolled over in the grass. When it rose and turned to run away, we hit it again. It fell, rose yet again, and ran on. At the edge of the clearing some three hundred yards away, the bear stood and looked back at us, then dropped on all fours and disappeared into the willows.

It had all happened in seconds. I could not remember how many times I'd fired. The previous night my rifle action was stiff with rust, requiring two hands to work the lever. Now I fired without effort.

"The bear initially stood up at the upper end of the meadow," Volk told us. "As I raised my camera, it dropped to all fours and ran at me! I tried to run but the tussocks tripped me so I lay still."

The dogs turned and ran back down the trail. That's when Ted saw the bear turn for the dogs, closing fast because the dogs' heavy packs slowed them down.

"That bear hear me and run! She know me," Johnny said. Among the four of us, only Johnny was not shaking uncontrollably. "I tell you, I dreamed bears when I was young. They never bother me."

We chained the dogs and reloaded our rifles. I had fired four times. My hands still trembled. Half way across the field we found a path of crimson blood fourteen inches wide.

"She not go far," Johnny predicted. We stalked with rifles ready. Eighty feet into the willows the bear lay crumpled. Relieved, I relaxed and moved toward it.

"You wait!" Johnny commanded. "Some man get killed that way. Bear not yet dead and make one try." He swept his hand as if it were a paw. He filled and lit his pipe as we waited in the stillness. He smoked. We watched. After a few minutes, Johnny said, "Okay now, bear dead." Still, he approached the grizzly slowly. He cocked his rifle and held it at arm's length with the muzzle at the base of the big skull. No motion. "Bear dead."

Conveniently we were near the creek and running water, dead trees were plentiful, and the ground was dry—a good place to camp. We gathered wood, started a fire, and went to skin the bear.

"Maybe four hundred pounds. Four or five years old," Johnny said. "You eat bear? Big potlatch. Fourth of July today!"

None of us had ever eaten bear meat. "How about you? You eat bear?" I asked.

"Maybe no good. If it eat some kind of root or any kind of meat, maybe too strong. Fort Yukon bear is no good, eat fish."

He began skinning but became disgusted when our steel knives dulled quickly. He sharpened his own Old Hickory knife quickly with a file and then joined Volk at the fire, leaving Ted and me to finish the work. It took us three hours to skin the bear, working carefully as we intended to keep the hide.

Johnny butchered the bear in forty minutes, placing ribs, hams, and organs on cut willows to keep them off the ground. Then he separated the vertebrae and gave Volk some of them to boil. For three days we slept and ate bear. The meat was tender and had no strong flavor. Tired of boiled bear, I fried some and started to take it off the fire.

"Cook more," Johnny said. He always gave us orders. Now I rebelled.

"I'll cook yours more but I eat mine this way."

"Okay. You be sorry. Lots of white man do that. Get sick. Never eat bear again."

Back on the fire went the meat until it was crisp. Thereafter we stuck with boiling. We would cook it around three hours. Volk learned to make bannock bread and became our baker. Yet another pot of meat would go on the fire; ribs hanging suspended in the smoke. We slept short stretches to awaken and eat again. Part of the meat we cut in strips to dry. Ted and I scraped and stretched the hide, which measured six feet long and was in good condition. We came to understand the foul odor of the outhouse at Gold Camp. That's what came of an almost pure meat diet.

"Tomorrow I go back to Gold Camp," Johnny announced. "I tell Sarah I only go for one week. Maybe Stanley go to Venetie. Sarah and boy in Gold Camp alone."

Johnny tried to tell me how to find his cabins at Ackerman Lake. We were deeply disappointed that he would not continue with us.

CHAPTER 6

Johnny Returns

The crackle of fire and Johnny singing in Gwich'in woke me. Johnny was in an excellent mood. I thought this was due to his decision to return to Gold Camp. Volk, Ted, and I were crammed into Volk's tiny tent to escape the light drizzle. Johnny had slept on his bed of blankets on a pile of willow boughs, having tied our ponchos above the mosquito netting to stay dry.

"I dream good last night! Old lady okay. I go Ackerman Lake with you."

Our spirits lifted; we would go on today. Ted and I hoisted the heavy wet bearskin high into a spruce where it hung, spread by willow poles. What was left of the bear meat we divided and packed, leaving the smoked ribs and drying strips hanging in the bushes. In three days we had eaten more than half the bear.

Johnny and Volk went ahead with the dogs. I waited impatiently for Ted to finish packing. The three of us had army-surplus pack frames called "mortar boards," made of wood and canvas. We placed kitchen sponges under the unpadded cotton shoulder straps at the point of contact. Still, with heavy loads, our arms would tingle at first, then throb, and in about twenty minutes go numb. The sequence reversed when we took the weight off our shoulders during a rest. Sometimes it was better to rest standing. We lashed gear to our pack frames. Ted did this in an untidy fashion that offended me. Usually I did not care to walk behind him. This time I did, fortunately, because Ted's blanket roll caught in the thick brush and fell to the ground without him noticing.

After walking several miles we came to a cache, a simple platform of logs built ten feet off the ground. Johnny pulled a ladder from the brush and climbed up to check his supply of matches, Off mosquito repellent, skin scrapers, pans, and other odds and ends. He took a frying pan, as he didn't care for our small aluminum pan. He found much of our gear to be "funny."

Bleached caribou antlers lay about the old campsite, which Johnny called *Git tsal* (Little Glacier) because ice covered a wide area here in winter. It lay in a broad pass, hills gently rising on either side. We caught grayling in the creek while Johnny set several wolf snares. As we went on, we saw many fresh tracks in the trail—moose, wolf, and bear.

"Bears fight here," Johnny pointed to freshly torn tundra. It was frightening to imagine the fierceness of the battle. Willows were torn from the ground. Large patches of moss were ripped and overturned in a patch twenty feet across. The newness of the disturbance left an unsettled feeling in my gut. We looked about uneasily.

When the trail filled with water we moved to higher ground along the hillside. Even here we encountered long fields of tussocks. I had a deep infection spreading around one big toenail. Ted had infected blisters in each instep. These made tussock walking even more tedious and painful but we did not complain.

Finally we stopped to camp. Chopped bear heart was soon boiling with rice and onions. Johnny walked off a ways. The mosquitoes were bad. My toe throbbed. Volk whined about the mosquitoes and, before I knew it, I rose from my heels, stepped through the fire, and grabbed Volk's collar at the throat.

"You God-damned Yankee! You complain one more time and I'll kill you!"

Volk offered no resistance. We settled into an uneasy silence, my anger glowing. I went to get water to put some distance between us. This explosion had been building for some while. Fortunately Volk and I had been through the plebe system together at The Citadel, building the strange bond the military system creates among classmates. We were somewhat inured to harsh words. Thereafter we became closer, forming a better team, each doing tasks without request, command, or rancor. There were no further complaints, and we never discussed this incident.

The next day the trail remained difficult. We reached a small creek in a willow flat. Johnny stopped at a narrow place. "No bridge," he said.

In wetlands Johnny pulled rubber overshoes over his moccasins. My left boot leaked from a hatchet cut. Ted's cheap boots were not waterproof. Ted, Volk, and I splashed through the creek, hauling dead trees from far around to build a bridge while Johnny sat by a fire, smoked his pipe, and drank tea. When the bridge was complete, Johnny crossed without comment, a little smile on his face. He was the only one with dry feet.

As we moved beyond the brush, the ground became firm and was covered with caribou lichen and later with scattered spruce. Our pace lightened. Easy walking! We came to a beautiful, clear lake surrounded by large spruce trees with hills rising several thousand feet in the distance. Ducks played on the water. We stopped to brew tea and found that the pot and box of tea had fallen from Diamond's pack. I was content to look for them on the way back, but Johnny repeated several times that he needed them.

Volk generously volunteered to search for the tea. I felt compelled to accompany him. We went back three miles and with some difficulty found the stream crossing where Johnny had made tea. No pot. On our return to join the others we took what we thought was a short cut and happened upon the pot with the box of tea still inside. It was a lucky find as Diamond had been off the trail. Tired, we silently handed the pot to Johnny and sank beside the fire to eat a duck he had shot and Ted cooked.

Johnny was not impressed with our find, though glad to get the tea back. "I don't think you find it. You don't know how." We did not admit our luck. We lay back to rest. Johnny passed a cigarette that Volk and I shared and began a story about another time the pack dogs had lost supplies.

"One time we were moving. All our gear was packed on the dogs. I just pack my rifle and a few things. Same with old lady. The dogs were hungry. Caribou ran across in front of us. Too fast! No time to shoot. The dogs took off after them. Early wintertime ... little snow on the ground and cold. Those dogs lose lots of gear and grub. I track maybe four or three days. I find everything."

You had snow to track in, I thought, but kept my mouth shut.

In late afternoon as we came to a long lake, Johnny announced, "*Van Nitsii,* Large Lake! Not far now!"

We walked along a well-worn trail around the lake to three small log cabins situated on a hill between Large Lake and Ackerman Lake beyond. What a welcome sight! The day was sunny and a slight breeze kept away the mosquitoes. Each lake was about five miles long. Large Lake had irregular shores with vegetation growing to the water's edge. Ackerman, though only a half-mile away, was oval with a wide gravel beach. Each lake drained from opposite ends. Johnny and his family had lived here for several years, leaving when the caribou no longer returned.

"Why do they call the other lake Ackerman, Johnny?"

"One time white man name Ackerman stop there with partner, prospectors, greenhorns. They know nothing. When ice first little strong, she go out too far. Maybe never see ice before and walk on it, then dance. Go out where ice too thin, fall through."

"What happened? Did he die?"

"Sure," Johnny responded.

Johnny had not been to his Ackerman Lake camp in some years. One reason for coming was to retrieve a large canvas wall tent. The largest of the three cabins was about nine by twelve feet and had a stove. The door was broken and inside everything was a mess. At first it appeared that a bear had done the damage. A sled, saws, axes, pans, basins, traps, snares, and lanterns were tumbled together on the dirt floor amid small amounts of tea, matches, tobacco, and nails. As Johnny checked around he discovered a few things missing—some Blazo fuel, five pounds of flour, fishhooks, canned meat, and a hammer, but he found the tent. It became obvious that humans were the culprits.

We straightened up the cabin and repaired the stove, windows, and door. A stack of split firewood that Johnny had stocked years before sat untouched. Soon we had a fire blazing in the stove with bear soup cooking. Our flour supply was gone and we had been looking forward to getting into the cache. To our dismay, we found the flour spilled across the floor, mixed with dirt and caribou hair. We salvaged around three pounds, carefully removing rodent droppings and hair. We occasionally found some of these "raisins" in the bannock bread we baked.

The doubled-over tent made a good floor covering. We made ourselves comfortable, ate, and played cribbage. How pleasant to be in this little cabin. Our irritations were gone, replaced by a sense of well-being and friendship.

The next morning was sunny but windy. Anxious to go fishing, Volk assembled his spinning rod, which Johnny had not seen before and thought was "funny." He fished with lures simply tied to a long line and tossed into the water.

"No use to fish today," he said. "Too much wind. No use."

Undaunted, Volk went down to the lake as Ted and I started breakfast. Within minutes Volk returned with an eighteen-inch lake trout. We were elated. Johnny said, "You lucky." Volk went back down to the lake, caught a large fish on the next cast, and brought it back triumphantly. Still Johnny said, "You lucky, that all," but with less assurance. The third fish brought Johnny to his feet asking, "How you do that?" He followed Volk to watch.

With lake trout on the menu, Johnny made bannock bread on a little fire outside, cooking it slowly. It was superior to the bread we cooked. Satiated, we lay in the grass basking in the sun and were soon asleep, awakening much later to find Johnny cooking. At the bear camp I had seen him pick up the bear's feet, which I discarded when we skinned the bear. I must have looked surprised to see them cooking in the broiler.

"Best part, the feet!" he smiled. Soon we all agreed.

By then some of the meat was spoiling. Ted and I cut away the worst parts to cook for the dogs. Johnny left to find a U.S. Geological Survey camp we had heard was set up on the lake the summer before. Volk returned to fishing. We caught more fish than we could immediately eat, so we made a rock enclosure at the lake's edge where we could store them for future meals.

In the evening Volk broke Ted's long winning streak at cribbage. Johnny lay back smoking, now and then mimicking their "fifteen-two, fifteen-four" chants as they counted points, shaking his head at the game. I read *A Hundred Best Loved Poems,* the only book I had brought. Next to the campfire Johnny fished glasses from his pack, carefully put them on, and asked to have a look. For an hour he worked his way through a poem here and there, finally returning the book to me with a nod of approval, saying, "Good. Just the same like Bible." I told him he could borrow it whenever he wanted.

"No, that's enough," he said. "That's enough. I never read anymore. Read Bible four times. After that, nothing, no more."

Finally we went to sleep about two or three in the morning. With all the July daylight our patterns shifted markedly. Johnny had already eaten by the time we arose. He surprised us with four eggs he had carried from Gold Camp. We matched coins. Volk won the extra egg. A fried egg was a luxury with broiled lake trout, bannock, and coffee.

"I dream maybe Sarah needs me. Maybe Stanley leave. I go today," Johnny announced.

The tent Johnny was taking back to Gold Camp weighed some forty pounds. It was too heavy for Diamond, the largest dog. Johnny cut out the tent's canvas end sections to pack on Blackie while I repaired rips in the dogs' packs. Volk brought up two large lake trout and a pike for Johnny to take with him; in return, Johnny gave each of us a piece of dry moose meat, enough oatmeal for one meal, and told us to use the remaining eight cups of flour. I handed him a heavy sewing needle and my poncho. Johnny's pack was much heavier going back.

Volk took a picture of Johnny, Ted, the dogs, and me. We wished Johnny a good trip. He hoped we would have a good stay in camp. I watched until Johnny and the dogs disappeared, going back the way we had come. How fortunate we were to have come across this wonderful old man. Still, we wanted time to ourselves. As Ted wrote in his journal at the bear camp, "Johnny always manages to find fault with everything that he did not help do, but I guess anyone eighty-one and still going as strong as he does is bound to be rather set in his ways."

GROWING UP I spent much time around elderly people, mostly women. I delighted in listening to their stories, which went back several generations, frequently to the times of the Civil War and the difficult postwar reconstruction in the South. Later I read the Bible and books about mythology and philosophy and thought a great deal about what this all meant. I was not sure if I was atheistic or agnostic. But I always found solace in the woods and had romanticized the naturalistic life of the Indian before the arrival of whites. Somehow in this old man everything came together. I remembered the expression on his face when I asked, "You believe in God?" We had been sitting on logs at Gold Camp during a break in the cabin work. His was looking down at the pipe he was filling. His eyes rose to meet mine. He lit the pipe, keeping his eyes on mine.

Exhaling smoke, he finally answered, "I see little tree—grow up. I see bird, animal, anything live—I see you. Sure, I know, there's the God."

This may not have been a biblical answer but it suited me just fine.

CHAPTER 7

Ackerman Lake

We explored the USGS campsite near Ackerman Lake. Johnny needed an oil drum from there for his camp. We found six or seven empty fifty-five-gallon drums and numerous five-gallon Blazo fuel cans and crates. Scrounging around we turned up two small C-ration cans of plum jam. Sweets were a rare treat. We drained the Blazo cans and consolidated several gallons of fuel for lanterns back at the cabin.

We struggled back to camp hauling the drum through rough terrain, brushy at the higher elevations and boggy in the lowlands. We tried several methods, finally suspending it from a pole with rope. After we got it to the cabin, I retrieved the last of the bear meat, which smelled pretty strong by then. Again I cut away the worst parts and made soup for supper.

Volk and Ted thought the soup was good but that I had added too much onion. After finishing the meal, I admitted that it had no onion at all, just aged bear meat.

For several days the sky had been gray with a light rain. Fishing was poor. I shot a duck but the wind carried it out into the lake. I was tempted to swim for it but doubted I could get out and back in this cold water. It was the only meat we wasted, and I regretted killing it.

The next morning, Volk went down to get a live fish for breakfast and discovered that they had escaped from our rock pool. Ted finally caught a pike. We spent most of the day making a raft of wooden crates and Blazo cans to extend our fishing range. The raft was large enough for one person. Ted took it out to deep water but caught no other fish.

There was supposed to be a second USGS camp somewhere on Ackerman Lake. Ted and I went with snares, rifles, and other gear to explore for rabbit trails and look for the government site. We saw no rabbit trails or other signs of game. Eventually we shot two ducklings, which turned out to be mostly feathers. It was a long day. We beat through the brush for hours but never found the other campsite and wearily returned to the cabin to make duckling soup, feeling we had accomplished little. Volk had caught fish for supper but we craved variety.

Volk made bannock and we boiled half of our remaining package of dried apples. He surprised us with a small package of sugar and one of dried cream, about what you would put into in a cup of coffee. He had hoarded these from Circle, much to our delight. Steamed apples over bannock with sweet condiments were such a luxury. Afterward we settled back in the bright lantern light and played cards, enjoying a camaraderie I still remember. We functioned well as a team, each of us spontaneously doing tasks as needed. Almost all the food we'd packed in was gone—coffee, tea, sugar, rice, and peas—but we were catching enough to eat. In fact, we were all gaining weight. Never being sure if we would catch food the next day inspired us to eat everything we caught and never waste it. And we still had a little flour and dehydrated eggs.

The next few days our luck changed; suddenly the fish were not biting. We spent many hours fishing, and Volk finally caught a forty-six-inch pike, the biggest we had seen. I was at the lakeside when it struck. Volk set the hook and expertly handled the fish. Each time he brought it near shore it would spook and dart back out to deep water. I waded out knee-deep as Volk led the fish back toward shore where I could grab it. It thrashed violently but I held on. The monster had battle scars across its back and its large mouth was full of razor-sharp teeth. We held the pike down on the beach and pounded it on the head until it was still.

After taking pictures of the monster pike, we fitted half of it into an old broiler and played cards while it cooked. We feasted on potatoes, bannock, and several platefuls of fish. This we washed down with Labrador tea, or Canadian tea as some called it, made from a plant Sarah had shown us. Boiling eight or ten twigs with attached leaves in a quart of water produced decent, rather pungent tea. Volk and I lay back lazily and smoked pipes while Ted took his turn washing up.

Fishing, cooking, and eating were our activities during the next week. We did not realize that a vitamin deficiency caused cuts to heal slowly and infect easily. Though our blisters and sore toes were much better, we were lethargic and had to force ourselves to replace the wood supply in the cabin before we left. Small green spruce grew near the cabins but dry standing dead trees were some distance away. These we found, cut, hauled, and sawed into firewood-sized pieces.

We never made it all the way to the west end of Ackerman Lake, five miles distant, where the outlet drained into the Middle Fork of the Chandalar. Nor did we make it to *Ch'idrii*, Heart Mountain, which Johnny had told us so much about and where he was sure we'd find Dall sheep. It had been one of his favorite hunting grounds.

JOHNNY HAD TOLD us he was *Di'haii Gwich'in*, the band that once lived in this area and to the west. Conflicts with inland Eskimos in the 1800s drove the *Di'haii* eastward to join the *Netsii Gwich'in* around Old John Lake and on the upper Sheenjek and Koness rivers. Johnny was born just south of Old John Lake, near the present site of Arctic Village, but his parents were *Di'haii*.

"That's bad people, Kobuk Eskimo. Fight too much," Johnny said, yet in general he expressed admiration for the Eskimos. He knew some Eskimo songs and stories and spoke some of their language, having traveled to their region and spent time with them. Commercial whalers and traders brought beads, tea, flour, tobacco, knives, guns, and cooking utensils to Barter Island and Hershel Island to exchange for furs and meat. The Eskimos traded goods to the Gwich'in.

European goods came to the Gwich'in through intertribal trading years before they encountered white people. Russian goods were available first, coming from southeast Alaska and trading posts on the lower Yukon River. In 1847, the Canadian Hudson's Bay Company built a trading post at Fort Yukon, then Russian territory. But the closest Russian trading post was hundreds of miles down the Yukon at Nulato. After the United States bought Alaska from Russia in 1867 the Hudson's Bay Company moved its trading post up the Porcupine River, once in 1869 and again soon thereafter into Canadian territory at Rampart House.

Johnny frequently told us stories of his younger days around the turn of the century.

"Used to be, we travel all over; never stay one place long time," he said. "We married in Fort Yukon, 1907. We go down on little steamboat ... William Loola, the first Native preacher, marry us and we come back up. Then we go up East Fork to Old John Lake. Sarah mother, father, too. Sarah mother die there. Nobody live at Arctic Village that time—just at Wind River, Smoke Creek, Junjik, all over.

"That time we got one metal pot, Russian. Three bolts hold bottom on. Heavy, too. Just one pack with little tea, flour. Before that we make hole in ground and put in skin or gut to hold water. Put rocks in fire, when hot put in water, boil meat.

"Just a few dogs that time. Summertime pack everything—look for food, see? In winter, use toboggan. Muzzle-loaded shotgun that time. Use caribou-skin blanket, tent. Sometime, no food. Not much white man food, that time. Just sometime little tea, flour. Just eat little meat, fish."

• • •

WE'D COME UP to Ackerman Lake in a roundabout way, around hillsides and lakes. Returning to Gold Camp we figured we could cut some mileage and save time by going straight over the mountain south of us. The trail quickly faded as we began to climb. We beat through thick willows to reach an almost bare mountain top covered with lichen, rocks, and ankle-high vegetation. The day was clear and the brisk wind felt good. The view was spectacular, overlooking the valley below and the hills stretching south to the horizon. To the north we looked back on Ackerman Lake and *Ch'idrii*, Heart Mountain. Beyond, waves of mountains extended west to east, filling the skyline. There was no human disturbance anywhere we could see—no noise, no air pollution. How I drank it all in!

We gobbled ripe cranberries. I sat with binoculars studying the land below, trying to pick the best route that avoided wetlands. Streaks of spruce were scattered among brushy open areas of willow and moss. This looked better than tussocks. I'd drained the abscess in my great toe as well as Ted's infected blisters. Our feet had healed and toughened. We got to the creek dry enough to take off our boots to wade across.

We stopped to make Canadian tea and rest. Our packs were light, and we were in better shape than we were when we set out from Gold Camp two weeks before. A mile and a half above *Git tsal,* the campsite that iced up in winter, we hit Johnny's trail, ankle deep in water but a better alternative than the thick brush on either side. We startled a grouse, and I shot it. We stopped a mile down the trail, in a dry spot near the creek, where Volk caught some grayling. Ted cleaned the grouse, then started a fire to boil it with rice. It was getting cold by then and would be dark for a few hours. Ted reached for the canteen, took a swig, and exclaimed, "There's ice in it!" A heavy frost was forming around us. We huddled close to the fire to dry our soaked feet and wait for sunrise.

Like hungry animals, we ate the boiled grayling, bones and all, and drank the broth. Then I bit into the grouse gizzard and felt a tooth crack. I expressed my displeasure that Ted had not known to clean out the gravel. Fortunately the tooth caused no problem. About four a.m. the sun returned, bringing with it some warmth. We had stopped at a good place to fish but a poor one to camp, so we moved a half-mile to *Git tsal.* We crowded into Volk's little tent with a fire out front and had a good sleep.

Volk rose early and returned to camp with a dozen grayling. We stacked them upright, crammed into the coffee can we used for a pot. We appreciated the ease of boiling and the benefit of the broth.

The brush was thick the last three miles to the bear camp, where we had left the skin to dry. We folded it and lashed it to my pack. With my hatchet, I extracted the four eyeteeth from the skull. Volk got the extra one, as he'd been the one who was charged by the grizzly. We gathered the remaining ribs and dry meat from the bushes and divided it among ourselves to eat along the trail. We crossed the tussock fields and grazed on blueberries as we hiked.

When Johnny walked along he occasionally broke over the top of a willow to mark the trail. We looked for those signs and found it useful to adopt the same habit.

We arrived at Six Mile Fork around midnight. The swift creek made a bend here with a large eddy. The ground was firm and dry with scattered spruce. Although long used as a campsite, it was not littered. A few items such as the little stove were stored in the trees for future use. Soon we had chopped bear ribs boiling, adding in the last of our rice and our last quarter of an onion. It cooked for several hours.

Later that day we continued walking downstream across gravel bars, following the creek through stretches of trees and finally made one last crossing. We were back at Gold Camp. Sarah, Stanley, and Lawrence greeted us. Johnny appeared with a bag of candy and shook our hands. Sarah fed us boiled dry bear meat, crackers, and tea.

Johnny had erected the big canvas tent he'd brought from Ackerman Lake. He helped us raise a smaller tent nearby and brought us blankets and tobacco. In my journal that day, I wrote, "I have never met a friendlier, more kindly, and unselfish person."

CHAPTER 8

Life in Camp

Early every morning, Stanley and Ted took the large canvas boat across the river to check their snares, frequently returning with seven rabbits. We fished daily. We ate rabbit soup or grayling at nearly every meal.

We spent most of our time working on the new cabin. We followed Johnny into the forest looking for straight trees about ten or twelve inches in diameter at the base. It was surprising to find such large spruce growing this far above the Arctic Circle. Johnny led us to a few downed trees that he had cut during the winter. These were limbed and cut to length, ready to drag to the cabin site. When Johnny found a standing live tree to his liking, we cleared brush around it to allow room to swing an ax. He identified several suitable trees and left us to cut them down. I preferred a well-used but solid double-bladed ax and kept it sharp. We had no power tools. We limbed the trees and cut the limbs to firewood length.

Then came the hardest work, moving the logs to the cabin site. Thick, sticky sap oozed from the green logs, which were much heavier than the dry ones. The mosquitoes were ferocious.

At the site we peeled the logs, lifting each one up while Johnny shaped and notched them until he was satisfied with the fit. Once the walls were up, we raised three large ridgepoles into position to support the roof. At right angles we closely fitted many wrist-sized poles to form the ceiling. Lawrence had gathered a huge pile of sphagnum moss, which we placed in a thick layer over the roof poles and covered with dirt, thus completing the roof.

Sarah often brought us tea and crackers. Johnny told stories during work breaks and later as we lay about lethargically in the tent after a hearty meal of rabbit soup or grayling with pilot bread, potatoes or rice, and tea. Often we listened to the radio, which was attached to a long antenna that brought good reception. Johnny and Sarah enjoyed KJNP, a religious station broadcasting from North Pole, near Fairbanks. Rev. Don Nelson, their favorite commentator, read or told Bible stories, occasionally reminding Johnny of his own Gwich'in stories.

"You know," Johnny told us, "Jesus not only one to die and come back again. One time Indian did that, too. *Dak Neehaa,* his name. He say, 'Pretty soon, I die. Put me on ice. In spring time I come back.' Well, he die. After, ice go out. By and by they hear singing. He come back, all dirty but wife clean him up. In a few years he do same thing. Die again, go out with ice, and come back. Even flies bother him, maggots too. But after come back everything okay. Eat good, tell story. He do that again. Last time say, 'This time I die, I not come back.'"

Then Johnny started a long story, told over several evenings, explaining, "Story like Samson, too."

K'aiiheenjik was a strong man, a real champion. He could lift a man by the nape of his neck with one hand. Two men could hold him, one on either side, but he'd get loose. He could jump a long way and run down a moose on snowshoes. Some Indians were jealous and killed his brother, with whom he was very close. Then a series of retaliations began. He trained his sister's two sons to help him. Many encounters took place, and he killed many people with a bone weapon, a spear, and a club made from caribou horn.

K'aiiheenjik and his nephews went away, trying to escape further violence but were followed and attacked. Both his nephews were killed. Many arrows struck *K'aiiheenjik,* too, but did not penetrate deeply. Finally *K'aiiheenjik* grew weary of the killing and climbed a high cliff. Two of his strongest enemies went up after him. He grabbed each of them around the neck and jumped off.

"Enemies die. *K'aiiheenjik* die too, but body not hurt, no change. Other two all broken up but he body, no scratch."

Johnny reminded us that Samson was killed when he pushed down the temple pillars; the bodies of everyone else were crushed but his body was intact with no sign of injury.

The story was very long. It was difficult to stay awake when you could not understand even the names of the principal characters and you'd worked hard all day, eaten a large supper, and laid back on spruce boughs.

I ENCOURAGED JOHNNY to make a moose-skin boat to go to Venetie, some forty or fifty miles downriver. He had mentioned several times that he would like to visit the village but was reluctant to go on foot. Of their fourteen children, four were still alive. Nathaniel, Hamel, and Maggie Roberts, Lawrence's mother, lived in Venetie. Dan Frank lived in Kotzebue where Jean, his wife, was a teacher. Johnny and Sarah had many grandchildren and great-grandchildren.

Johnny had intrigued me with his talk about skin boats. I wanted to make one. We had finished the heavy work on the cabin. Just the door, windows, and floor remained. Johnny had cut the floorboards. Stanley agreed to stay with Sarah if Johnny went downriver to Venetie.

When a heavy rain struck suddenly, the big tent leaked badly. We placed the ponchos and Volk's ground cloth over the top. After the rain, Stanley started a fire in the outside stove. We drank tea and listened to Johnny. He'd not been down the river in a skin boat in eighteen years. He talked of the problems he visualized.

"Some places lots of channel. Fast water, too. Tree, too, danger in water."

"Any rapids or rocky areas?" I asked.

"No, that is upriver, below Arctic Village. Big danger there." By the time we went to bed it seemed likely that we'd make the boat.

"Maybe eighteen feet with three skins would be okay," Johnny announced at breakfast.

We would make a boat! Ted and Stanley went to check their snares and returned with three large and four young rabbits. Johnny walked downriver to recover a dried moose skin he'd left at a kill site, rolled up and stored in a nearby spruce tree. There were two skins in the cache. Sarah sat on the ground patiently trimming the hair from the skins with scissors, starting in the middle and working outward in circles.

"If leave hair on, get wet, too heavy; hold too much water," Sarah said.

Sarah put the skins into a washtub to soak and then cleaned the rabbits and put them in a pot on the stove to boil. I took a rare warm-water sponge bath and washed my clothes. Johnny returned with the moose skin and eleven grayling.

"Pretty near I don't find it. Maybe two years ago I shot that moose."

In the evening we walked upriver. For a boat frame, Johnny selected several long, slender trees twenty-two to twenty-four feet long and three to four inches in diameter at the butt, tapering to an inch and a half at the top. After supper he demonstrated how to make planks. First he carefully trimmed all the branches so you could move your hand smoothly over the trunk. Then he nailed each end to a large anchor log that he'd cut a slice off of lengthwise by whipsaw. He straddled the log and cut down the length of the pole with an ax, creating a flat side. Finally he rotated the pole 180 degrees, re-nailed it, and cut the opposite side. The finished plank was an inch and a half thick.

There were two anchor logs. Stanley and I spent the next afternoon making planks, his six to my three. Ted and Stanley had seen fresh moose tracks across the river. Johnny went over to hunt but did not find the moose. In the evening we again stuffed ourselves with fried rabbit, boiled grayling, rabbit soup, stewed apples, biscuits, coffee, and tea.

Johnny was in a jovial mood, smoking his Pederson pipe and gesturing with his hands as he spoke. "Well, I tell you, lots of *Vasaagihdzak* stories. Another one too—*Ch'iteehaakwaii*, he's like the Jesus. He go all over and help people. His name means 'He Paddles Canoe.' Crow stories, too." He laughed, "Lots of stories.

"Remember, I tell you, all animals, everything, used to be, speak one language; bear, bird, people, everything. Long time ago, I don't know how many thousand years, lots of giants, big animals, eat people. *Vasaagihdzak, Ch'iteehaakwaii* help people, make animals so they can't grow big.

"*Vasaagihdzak* needed feathers for arrows. He go, climb up, find big nest. Just little eagles in nest. He ask them, 'Where you parents?'

"'They go hunt.' *Vasaagihdzak* wait. By and by, mother eagle come back with man's leg, arm too. *Vasaagihdzak* use short spear, got sharp horn on end. Kill eagle. He wait again. When father come back with man's body, he kill that one, too.

"*Vasaagihdzak* tell little eagles, 'Go get ground squirrel.' They do it.

"When they come back, he tell them, 'Now you never grow big! Just eat small animal like ground squirrel. Never eat man.'"

We drank tea, smoking our pipes. Stanley asked, "Ackerman Lake, you see anything? Maybe big fish or snake live there. One time caribou were swimming across, maybe twenty-five or thirty. Something just swallow them up. Nothing left."

Johnny asked, "I tell you how crow get sun?"

A shake of my head and Johnny goes on.

"At that time the day was short and the night long. Well, bear want it dark all the time. Lots of all kind of animals don't want it dark, see? Fox want half daylight. When dark come fox holler, 'Go back to daylight.' Then half day and half night.

"Bear get mad and try to make it dark but he can't do it. So bear take sun," Johnny reaches up, as if lifting it from the sky, and laughs, "and hang it inside his skin house. Now only bear got sun. Everybody else, no sun, just dark.

"They tell crow, 'We need sun.'

"Crow smart. Smart as man, used to be. Well, he fly up, look for light but find nothing.

"Crow tell bear, 'My uncle, we go in your house.'

"Well, they go in and crow tell 'em some kind of big story. Crow fly everywhere, got all kind of stories.

"The sun is hanging right there, in bag.

"Bear got one daughter, good-looking. Bear jealous, won't let girl see man so nobody can marry her.

"Crow tell that girl, 'Come, we go drink water.' Crow and daughter go to a little creek to drink water. Clear water. Crow try it. 'By golly, tastes good!'

"Crow make himself small, a little dark thing, like little feather or spruce needle. Daughter start to drink, but when she lean over see that little black something in water." Johnny gestures pulling back his head. "Every time start to drink, she see that little black thing.

"Finally she drink. Little black thing go inside. That's crow.

"Well, she get pregnant, see?" Johnny laughs, as do Sarah and Stanley. Lawrence, too, is listening. Johnny has our complete attention.

"Baby grow fast. Pretty soon born. Little boy. Grow fast, too. One day, start to crawl. Next day play, start to walk.

"Bear keep sun in bag. Little boy see that and start to cry, 'Grandpa, give me that,' pointing to the bag.

"'No,' bear say.

"Little boy cry lots. 'Grandpa, give me that!'

"'No!' But bear like grandson too much, so finally give in and give 'em sun. 'Just play inside. Don't go outside.'

"Little boy happy," Johnny gives a big smile and gestures, "He roll sun all around on floor. By and by he go near door and quick, go out. Bear can't stop him.

"Crow grabs sun and throws it up in the air. Bear mad, chase him, but boy change to crow and fly away. Animals all happy. Everybody got light!"

We all laughed. "Well, lots good story. I tell you."

We snuggled into our pile of blankets as I went to sleep thinking about our experiences. I had envisioned just the three of us camping, hiking, and living off the land, but the trip had become a far different and richer experience. Silently I thanked Chief Christian for directing us to Gold Camp and to Johnny and Sarah Frank.

Later I learned it was possible that the Gwich'in lived in northern Alaska at the same time as large prehistoric animals, during the Pleistocene era, which ended about ten thousand years ago. This area was amazingly ice-free at a time when glaciers covered much of the Arctic. Among many species were woolly mammoths, giant sloths, saber-toothed cats, short-faced bears, huge beavers, and a nine-foot salmon. *Aiolornis incredibilis,* an eagle with a sixteen-foot wingspan, once flew the Pleistocene skies of what became the American West. Archeological evidence of man's presence in Gwich'in country included finds in Chalkyitsik, near Fort Yukon, estimated to be ten thousand years old, and stone and bone tools in the Bluefish Caves near Old Crow, Yukon Territory, that are even older by as much as ten thousand years.

After breakfast, we went with Johnny to look over our new planks. He didn't like most of them and muttered, "*Gwinzuu* (it's bad)," to himself. Johnny headed off to the downriver cache for nails. Ted went across the river with Stanley, again using the large canvas canoe to cross the main channel. The river still ran fast though the level had dropped in the past month. The trails were dry now.

Stanley told Ted, "I dreamed I would catch five rabbits today."

He got five. Ted's snares yielded two. It was a good year for rabbits near the height of a ten-year cycle for snowshoe hares. Predators that ate them cycled, too, increasing along with their food supply. Soon the hares would overpopulate and then crash.

Lawrence asked me to go with him to check his snares, which were not far from the tents. His four snares were empty. He made adjustments to each one. We picked blueberries, as yet scarce around Gold Camp, and set four more snares. A tree squirrel chattered.

"Can I shoot it?" he asked.

"To eat?"

"For the dogs."

"Sure, if Johnny says okay."

Lawrence fetched the .22 rifle from camp, checked the chamber and barrel, and then loaded a cartridge, careful to point the rifle away from us. I was impressed with his gun handling. He waited until he had a clear view and shot the squirrel.

Despite his young age, Lawrence made fires, used a knife and ax skillfully, and made and set snares. He packed water, worked on the cabin, and cooked. In my journal I wrote, "Have never seen anything like it. He never complains, fusses, frets, or even frowns." The boy received quiet approval back at the tent.

"*Gwinzii* (good)," Sarah spoke in her low soft voice, smiling. "Put in dog food. *Gwinzii.*"

Sarah sat on folded canvas working with the skins of three cow moose that had soaked overnight.

"Best one for boat is bull moose, August or September—thick one, strong too," Johnny told us. "These all winter skins. Give me you canvas, you brother, too. I need it."

"Me, too. I need it to keep my blanket dry!" I responded.

Johnny stood quietly, looking at me. I turned and stalked to our gear. I snatched up the two pieces of canvas and took them to him. He smiled and stretched them out. "We need for boat," he said.

Sarah examined the skins carefully and scraped off remnants of flesh. We stretched the skins, straining in a tug of war under Johnny's watchful eye. He roughly measured each one with his hands. "Eighteen feet. Make boat eighteen feet, it's okay."

Hour after hour Sarah sewed the skins tightly together so as to be waterproof. Occasionally she stopped to stretch and relax her hands. Johnny and Stanley cut and prepared more planks. Johnny admonished Stanley to "go slowly and make a good one." I was pleased that two of my planks were among the best five used for the floor. I cooked lunch: boiled rabbits, rice and onions, bannock doughnuts, and blueberries.

After lunch we began constructing the frame. We used five planks for the floor, two of them with the narrow end to the stern and three to the bow. These we arched and tied with rope using a stout piece of wood as a fulcrum and increasing the tension to obtain the proper shape. We cut short planks for the ribs, three across the bottom and sides and one at each end. Gradually the frame took shape, becoming a nicely shaped scow, upswept at bow and stern. Two planks completed the sides, which leaned out at an angle. I had serious doubts that we would ever be able to cover the frame with the skins we had. Yet Johnny seemed unconcerned. We added three narrow seats that also served as braces. The completed frame was esthetically pleasing and very sturdy. We stopped to eat supper that Lawrence prepared while we worked—rabbit still our main course.

Sarah had sewed our canvas to the skins. We strained and stretched. Gradually the skins and canvas were made to cover the length of boat, just lapping over the bow and stern crossbars. We attached it with small nails. I remained skeptical until the last moment. Johnny was not surprised by the perfect fit and made no comment. Then we stretched the wet skins sideways to lap over the gunnels. Again the fit was nearly perfect. The finished scow was eighteen feet long, three and a half feet wide at the middle, tapering toward the ends, and a foot and a half deep. The bow swept up more gradually than the stern. I was impressed. Johnny was quietly pleased.

Johnny and Stanley left to cut a straight-grained, dead standing tree to make a pilot paddle. "I know good one," Johnny said. "Just right. Save it long time. Someday good paddle."

Stanley carried back a seven-foot section. Johnny roughed out the shape with an ax, then went to work with my hatchet and a "crooked knife" to shape the paddle, creating a large pile of curled shavings. Using his thumb on the curved knife blade as a gauge, he drew the crooked knife toward himself, hardly looking down. The paddle shaft became oval and the blade a lazy diamond on cross-section with a tapered middle ridge. The tip had a broad V-shape and the upper end tapered to fit his hand.

"Pilot paddle," Johnny announced as he stood to demonstrate its use and then held it out to me. It was smooth with no burrs. I was delighted to witness his skill. Johnny had finished the paddle in less than an hour.

I examined the curved blade of his crooked knife, its handle worn smooth from many years' use.

Johnny said, "Hudson Bay."

"What you mean?"

"Old Hudson Bay scissor. Old one," he smiled.

• • •

THE NEXT MORNING was cloudy and raining.

"No chance today," Johnny said. "Weather bad. We wait."

I went with Lawrence to check his snares. He caught a rabbit. We took up the snares. At camp we put the ponchos and ground cloth over the tent again. Volk put away tools and sorted gear. I helped Teddy and Stanley carry the skin boat over to the main channel for the maiden voyage. The boat handled quite nicely. They returned with four rabbits.

We spent the afternoon lying on the boughs in the tent. Johnny passed tobacco to Volk and me and told stories as we smoked our pipes. In the background peaceful music played on the radio. A brilliant rainbow appeared across the valley; one end seemed to come right to Gold Camp.

Johnny laughed. "This is gold treasure at end of the rainbow!"

After supper we listened to "Trapline Chatter" on KJNP, a ritual for Johnny and Sarah. This daily program aired personal messages and offered the only communication available for people in remote areas of Alaska. The messages might include news of the birth of a baby, announcement of visitors, and whatever other information people felt the need to pass along. Rarely were the messages pertinent to Johnny and Sarah but occasionally they recognized names.

Johnny allowed us to take the radio to our tent to listen for news of a manned spacecraft launch on July 21. The launch was delayed many times. Finally we no longer could keep our eyes open. We awoke to hear that the mission had been successful. Gus Grissom was propelled in a Mercury craft to 126 miles above the earth, becoming the second American astronaut in space. The sixteen-minute suborbital flight took place three months after the Russian cosmonaut Yuri Gagarin became the first human in space.

THE DRONE OF a plane grew steadily louder as we ate breakfast. Soon the invasive but welcome sound reverberated in the valley. We watched the plane approach, first flying low over the landing strip to check it out, then swooping over the tents and back around again to land. After bumping to a stop and swinging about, the pilot and four passengers climbed out onto the gravel bar. Johnny recognized Keith Harrington, the Wien pilot. Stanley and I took the new skin boat over and brought back Johnny and Sarah's daughter Maggie, who was holding a baby, and two young children and a second woman. I went with Johnny to talk with Keith. Johnny paid him fifty dollars for the flight from Venetie. Stanley was ready to get back to the village and quickly packed to catch a ride with Keith.

In the afternoon we cut firewood, hauled water, and brought over Maggie's gear.

"Nobody needs Venetie fire crews this year, so not much money," Maggie said. "Store got no flour, rice, sugar. People are in bad shape."

Maggie was in her mid-twenties, the youngest of Johnny and Sarah's children. Framed by coal-black, shoulder-length hair, her face resembled Johnny's with high cheek bones. She spoke quietly and at first seemed shy. The three children were hers, and Lawrence was her oldest child.

Sarah cooked a hundred or so biscuits and doughnuts to send downriver with Johnny in the new boat. He packed some basic grub and dry meat. We carried gear to the boat, which had been pulled out of the water, its skin covering dry and as tight as a drum. Earlier I'd put it in the water to soak. The skin expanded when wet and I needed slack to repair a hole with sinew Sarah had given me. Volk had pulled it up on the shore, unaware of my intentions. We put the boat back into the water and went back to camp for more tea.

Sarah wanted my hatchet. I was quite attached to it but could not refuse her. We also gave her a poncho, bandages, and a few other things. Ted and Volk took pictures. Sarah tried to give me a parka she made, which Johnny was taking to sell in Venetie. It had a heavy cotton shell with duck feathers and down stuffing with a fur ruff. Accepting the parka did not feel right.

At 4:15 p.m. we shoved off. The evening was cold with a stiff breeze blowing upriver. I sat in the bow, Ted and Volk were in the middle, and Johnny stood in the stern so he could see ahead to pick the route. We went down the slough and entered the fast current of the main channel. Ted and I tried to paddle steadily to keep warm, but Johnny objected.

"No paddle. I tell you when," he said.

Once, when I attempted to head for what appeared to be the most favorable route, he stopped me, then turned to consult with Volk. "Rick, what you think?" Finally Johnny would say, "That way," pointing or nodding his head.

Then we would paddle furiously across the river, barely making it to the desired channel, but warming ourselves with the exertion. A few miles downriver, all the channels came together as the river squeezed between high hills on one side and *Ddhah Dzak,* a dark, forbidding mountain, on the other. After three or four hours we stopped to make tea and eat dry meat and biscuits. Johnny took out the biscuits reluctantly, wanting to save them for Venetie. The sun was hidden behind the hills and it grew colder on the river. I pulled out Sarah's parka and thereafter only my hands, legs, and feet were cold.

We continued downriver as more channels opened up, and again Johnny expressed uncertainty. "By golly, I don't know, too many channel. What you think, Rick?"

After a delayed decision was made, we dashed for the chosen channel and the brisk paddling warmed us again. Around midnight we passed the junction of the north and middle forks of the Chandalar River. A high bluff here, where giant eagles once lived, was the last high country as we headed downriver. A beautiful sunset lasted several hours. For the first time since well before solstice it was dark enough for a star to appear.

We stopped again, and Johnny quickly made a blazing fire. Usually one of us started the fire, but Johnny was cold and we were "too slow—funny," he said. After eating, Johnny appeared ready to cast off—too soon, we thought—so we began plying him with questions about the early days. As he told stories, we gathered wood to keep the blaze going and managed to extend the stop. Two hours later, just as we were starting to doze off, Johnny announced it was time to go.

The wet skins flopped against the frame in the waves. After the first hour, Volk frequently bailed with a cup, as there was constant seepage, but the boat handled well and we felt secure. In the low country the river spread into the Yukon Flats with many channels. In places the channel was so shallow that we dragged on the river bottom—barely so, but enough to worry us. Sometimes the main channel narrowed and was cluttered with "sweepers"—trees that had been undercut by the current and fallen into the river. Now we understood what Johnny meant when he warned, "Tree is danger, too." The rapid current passed through the branches, some of them submerged, and swept us toward them. We paddled hard to avoid catastrophe.

We arrived in Venetie about 6:30 a.m. on July 22, fourteen hours after leaving Gold Camp. We packed our gear up to Hamel and Mary Franks' cabin where Hamel greeted his father and fixed breakfast for us. We ate sparingly as their cupboards were bare. When we began to doze off, Hamel took us out to his cache to sleep. There was no food in the cache so we had lots of room. It was obvious how hard things were.

Stanley woke us around noon. "The teacher has a radio," he said. "Maybe you can ask him to make a call for you to get a plane to Circle."

He walked us over to the teacher's home and introduced us to Dick and Mildred Birchell and their five children—David, Debby, Sharon, Bruce, and Jeffrey, who ranged in age from one to fourteen. They invited us in for coffee, served in china cups with saucers. Mrs. Birchell offered "leftovers," which we politely refused. When her probing questions uncovered the fact we'd not had lunch, she insisted we eat. And did we ever! We consumed ham, fried chicken, corn, greens, bread, butter, cheese, jelly, potato salad, cranberries, blueberry pie, tapioca pudding, tea, and coffee. We had missed vegetables. As we ate and ate and then ate some more, Mrs. Birchell seemed to take our hunger in stride and kept putting out more food.

As we talked, a Wien plane passed over the village. David Birchell, the oldest son, went up to the airstrip where he learned that the pilot already was headed for Fort Yukon so he would charge us only twenty dollars each to go on from there to Circle. We asked for a little time to say our good-byes before leaving.

First, we went to Abraham Christian's cabin to let the chief know we were okay and to retrieve a few things we'd left there. Halfway across the village we met him coming to find us. Ted took a photograph of Abraham in front of his fully grown potato plants. Then I hurried to Hamel's cabin, where Johnny sat around with his son and several other men. They made no effort to move. Johnny said we owed him eighteen dollars for the trip—six dollars each. If I wanted the skins it would be extra.

"How much?" I asked.

"Twenty-five dollar."

"Twenty-five more? Can I take the pilot paddle?"

"No, for everything. You can take the paddle."

I paid him, then hurried down to the river to remove the moose skins. I rolled them up, wet and slimy, and then I returned to Hamel's cabin. We said goodbyes. Days before at Gold Camp I'd asked how to say goodbye in Gwich'in. Johnny had not answered immediately but seemed to think about it before speaking. "*Shanandaii*—you remember for me. *Nineechaldaii*—I remember for you."

I stood. Johnny and the other men sat. Somewhat baffled, I left. Almost everyone in the village had come to the airstrip when we arrived. Now no one saw us off. It gave me an odd feeling.

Off we flew, passing back over the village before heading south. I pressed my head to the window, not only to watch the sinuous curves of the small creeks below but also to hide my face. Tears streaked down my cheek as I told myself, *Nineechaldaii*—I remember for you. How could I ever forget?

We arrived at Circle around 6:30 p.m. and stuffed ourselves with candy as we talked with Frank Warren in his store. "Some guy tried to sleep in your jeep but I ran him out—sent him to the church to sleep."

I'd forgotten to tell Mister Warren about Bill Bennett. There was a note from Bennett in the jeep, written on a napkin and stuck over the gearshift. He'd arrived July 1, having stopped in Seattle to visit his brother on his way north. Hitchhiking had been good all the way.

Mister Warren gave us a tow with his tracked "weasel" as the jeep battery was dead. It cranked easily when we got moving. We bought fifteen gallons of gas and a quart of oil for $10.70; my journal notes these "high prices" with an exclamation mark. Mister Warren did not charge us for keeping an eye on the jeep.

Heading south down the dusty Steese Highway toward Fairbanks, we spotted more than two hundred rabbits in the first eighty miles. Their feet had turned white already, changing color for winter camouflage. Soon they would be completely white.

In Fairbanks, we camped on the grounds of the Tanana Valley Fair, where we met Mr. and Mrs. Chappell, a retired couple from east Texas—"rice farmers," we were told. Mrs. Chappell was a birder with more than five hundred birds on her life list. She had guided Roger Tory Peterson in their region when he was collecting data for his book, *Birds of Texas*. They traveled with a small well-kept Airstream trailer that they pulled behind a large Cadillac. We enjoyed trading stories.

We visited the Klepacs, with whom we had a mutual friend in South Carolina. Mr.

Klepac was a master sergeant in the army stationed at nearby Fort Wainwright. We'd visited the family in June and were invited to return. On our way we stopped at a gas station where we bathed one by one in the restroom. At the Klepac trailer we munched cookies. Their daughter arrived from a church picnic and announced the leftovers would be served at the Calvary Baptist Church that evening.

"You're welcome to come," she said.

"These are our best clothes," I responded. We looked very scruffy.

"That's okay," Sergeant Klepac said.

We chatted outside with members of the church between a Sunday school program for the young people, including us, and the regular sermon. We followed the others back in and found ourselves in the choir section. There was no retreat. We sat behind the preacher, a missionary recently arrived from Japan, where he'd been "working to bring those people to Jesus and the Lord God." The church was fundamental in tone and intent. Attendees partially filled the benches in front of us. We sat on elevated tiers and received a thorough scrutiny. We had to appear attentive. One man sat alone in the center of the second row from the front. He dozed periodically, to awaken, cough, and say, "Amen, brother, amen." Then he'd fall asleep again, slowly sprawling and slumping.

Finally the service was over. The picnic leftovers, our enticement to attend, were a feast to us—sandwiches, salads, cookies, cakes, punch, tea, and coffee. We made the most of it, receiving much encouragement to "finish it up."

The next day we reorganized ourselves and went shopping. After mailing a box of food, tobacco, and candy to Johnny and Sarah, we enjoyed dinner at the Klepacs. We were very food-oriented after our time in Gwich'in country. Sergeant Klepac gave us rice and sixteen large cans of army C-rations. He also gave Ted and me closely shorn haircuts. Volk wisely declined.

In his journal, Teddy wrote, "We figured up everything except the gas. I have spent $45 on plane rides, $6 for the trip in the skin boat, $15 for a parka, $46 for food, generator, voltage regulator (jeep repairs) etc. This adds up to $112. I have also spent $12 on junk food. I will have to be more careful! The gas comes to about $40 each so far. I could kick myself for spending $12 and also for gaining thirteen pounds! I now weigh 141 pounds. I am too fat."

We visited Denali National Park (then known as McKinley Park) on the way to Anchorage. At the park I asked a ranger about the bearskin. He'd just given a talk on bears. I explained our circumstances and described the dried skin. The bearskin was about six feet square and medium brown except for a broad blonde area down the back.

"Well, if I were to see a hide like that, I'd say grizzly, but without a license or tag, I'd have to report it. Keep it wrapped up. Bear hides are not supposed to leave the state without a tag."

At the Canadian border the customs agent wanted to know if we had enough cash to get through Canada. Volk had less than two dollars. Ted and I each had about one hundred dollars. We convinced him that we would not become a burden on Canada.

The agent also asked about the moose skins that we had rolled up and tied to the front bumper.

"They were old skins used for a boat," I explained, saying nothing about the bearskin. He waved us through.

CHAPTER 9

Back Home

Back in South Carolina I felt closed in, controlled by society and family. In Alaska I felt unrestricted, free. Ted and I had been home a few days. Showered and well trimmed, I offered to drive to the hospital with my father for daily rounds. Frequently one of us accompanied him.

"Not like that, you're not. Shave that beard first."

I did as he demanded and went with him. Pop had been supportive of my travels and fostered our independence. Mother was loving and protective. She wanted us to stay home.

Medical school demanded most of my time. My relationship with a young teacher was frustrating. I cared for her, but her goal was marriage and suburbia and these were visions of our future that I did not share. We broke up but were back together by Thanksgiving as I succumbed to a regulated life again.

It was my good fortune the previous spring to have met David Youngblood, a classmate. He was scraping old paint off a small seaworthy dinghy propped on sawhorses under the dorm. I dropped my books and pitched in to help. David's face was tanned and his posture erect, his speech was precise and emphasized with hand gestures. Soon we became friends and spent much time together in the little boat on the waters around Charleston. Having grown up in Beaufort among low-country marshes and waterways, David introduced me to the world of tides and saltwater marshes.

The second year of medical school was mostly boring. The excitement and pressure of the freshman year was gone, as was the mystique. Introductory lectures on a variety of medical subjects were easy to read in a book or in a classmate's notes. We were not yet seeing patients. David had returned the borrowed dinghy. We were restless.

In midwinter David appeared at my dorm door with good news.

"A guy in Beaufort said we could use his metal hull twelve-foot lifeboat for the next few years," David said. "We could bring it up this weekend."

We brought the lifeboat sixty miles up the Intracoastal Waterway from Beaufort to Charleston with a one-and-a-half horsepower British Seagull motor. It was a slow, cold trip on a dark, moonless weekend in mid-January 1962. We had come two-thirds of the way by the second night when about two in the morning we sighted a large bonfire lighting the shore ahead. We pulled in and joined three men standing around the blaze.

"Where you boys going?"

"Charleston."

"Pretty slow trip with that little motor, ain't it?"

"Yeah, but it's okay, just cold."

"Care for a swig? Help warm you up." One of the men passed a bottle around. "We been fishing. No luck tonight."

The threesome got together often, a white and two black Gullah men. Gullahs were brought to these coastal islands as slaves generations before and spoke a distinct dialect. These men depended on the crabs, fish, and deer they caught for food to supplement their meager incomes.

"Might as well let the fire burn down. Sure you boys don't want a ride to town?"

After a glance between us, Youngblood said, "We'll take you up on that."

"Better give you a hand getting that boat above the tide line."

We crowded into their old car and helped finish the bottle on the way to Charleston.

A QUARTER-MILE FROM our dormitory, a short walk carrying oars and the outboard motor, was the boat harbor, our gateway to a different world. I learned about tides, currents, and wind as we rowed or motored in Charleston Harbor. Either we would go three miles out to Fort Sumter—site of the first battle of the Civil War—or follow the tidal rivers and creeks.

David had a friend whose family owned more than ten thousand acres in the wild, relatively undisturbed low country areas of black-water swamps, coastal islands, and forests hung with Spanish moss. It was a welcome escape from the confines of medical school. At night we poled a plank boat in the swamp hunting bullfrogs, the red eyes of young alligators reflecting in our spotlight. We chased raccoons in the marsh at low tide. A pint of applejack whiskey was a necessary precursor to eating raccoon roasted on a palmetto frond over an open fire. When the outer portion burned, we'd cut off a piece and chew the charred meat while the next layer cooked.

We were barely getting by in our classes and once in a while we thought about dropping out of school. David and I had entered medical school after just three years of college; if we quit, we would be left with no degree, so we talked ourselves into finishing the year. I accepted a summer externship at Self Memorial Hospital in Greenwood, South Carolina. It offered good clinical experience and an opportunity to work with my father.

In the spring we began to go into the hospital wards. I met a patient with a gaudy, heavy gold watchband marking him as an Alaskan. He convinced me that summer jobs were plentiful in Alaska and easy to get. I wrote Dr. Hunter May in Greenwood to renege on my externship. He understood and described my nature as "peripatetic." I had to look up the word—"a person who travels from place to place." My father was not pleased, but remained supportive and offered the jeep for a second summer. He considered this to be my last fling.

Ted was all for going to Alaska again. I decided to invite Willy Carpenter, a friend from high school and The Citadel, who was finishing his first year of medical school. In our mid-teens Willy and I had hiked more than two hundred miles together at Philmont Scout Ranch in New Mexico.

When I called to ask if he wanted to go to Alaska to find seasonal jobs, Willy's immediate response was, "When do we leave?"

OUR PACE WAS slow, as it had been the previous summer. We averaged a little better than thirty miles an hour, stopping to camp outdoors and fixing all our own meals. West of Cheyenne, Wyoming, my spirits rose as we approached the Rockies. Clouds hid the Tetons. Yellowstone was snow-covered and beautiful. Old Faithful erupted with a cloud of steam. It was cold but this time we had sleeping bags. Willy and I had new lightweight down bags. Ted had an old army-surplus bag, emerging every morning decorated with feathers. What a pleasure it was to sleep warm.

In Montana, I called home from a phone booth. I'd passed my classes. At the border an officer sealed our rifles with a wire and lead device to prevent their use as we passed through Canada. The .22 rifle was a takedown model. With the loosening of one screw, the rifle could be separated easily into two pieces and the wire slipped off. Rabbits were again plentiful and supplemented our diet.

In Anchorage, we looked up Claude and Alma Rhoades. Alma was the sister of "Uncle" Albert, a friend of my parents from World War II. The Rhoades were warm, open people who told good stories about their life in Alaska. She had cooked on a commercial fishing boat for many years. We stayed in a guest trailer near the Rhoades' home, met their friends, toured Anchorage, and were well cared for.

The new Providence Hospital was due to open in August 1963. I inquired about an externship at the old hospital and got a quick rejection from an administrator who made it clear that no students, interns, or residents worked there.

We went to the Kenai Peninsula for a fishing weekend at the Rhoades' cabin on the fast-moving, glacier-fed Kenai River. On Sunday morning Claude sent me to buy a bottle of vodka, assuring me that the bar at Moose River would be open. I was doubtful but found the bar open at nine o'clock. Already a few quiet customers sat scattered about the dark barroom. The drink before them seemed to be of the "hair-of-the-dog-that-bit-you" variety.

In Seward, we walked the docks in the boat harbor, surrounded by snowcapped mountains. White glacial fingers separated groves of dark timber. Resurrection Bay, long and narrow, extended out to the Gulf of Alaska, out of sight beyond the bends. Commercial and sport fishermen and their families landed, unloaded, and cleaned their boats. Claude bought a fresh-caught halibut for thirty-five cents a pound.

In the evening, Claude and I cut halibut steaks for dinner and prepared the rest of the fish for freezing in water to prevent freezer burn. Alma cooked the steaks, introducing us to the wonderful flavor of fresh halibut.

Back in Anchorage, we washed dishes, weeded the Rhoades' lush garden, and worked on an apartment building the couple owned. We looked diligently for regular paying jobs, too.

Willy and I made an appointment with Dr. Kazusai Kasuga at the Alaska Native Medical Center, a federal facility run by the U.S. Public Health Service. Doctor Kasuga, a pleasant and charming man, told us the center's two summer externships had been filled. He showed us around the clinics and hospital. Doctor Kasuga explained that federal health care for Native Americans was granted in federal treaties with Indian nations in the lower 48 states. Later, this service was extended to Alaska's Indians, Eskimos, and Aleuts, although they had neither signed any treaty with the U.S. government nor negotiated a settlement for the taking of their lands.

"We have regional hospitals around the state," he said. "This hospital is the referral hospital for all of them."

I offered to work for room and board but there was no opening. We visited federal and state agencies but all openings for seasonal work had been filled. The Alaskan I met in the hospital in South Carolina had been mistaken. We should have applied before coming.

Enough trying to be responsible, I thought, and suggested we fly to Venetie and go upriver to Gold Camp. Ted and Willy agreed. During the winter we'd kept in touch with Johnny and Sarah, and with the Birchells in Venetie. My mother had sent boxes of books for the school library. Occasionally we sent supplies to Johnny and Sarah, too, and received beadwork in return.

We drove to Fairbanks where we camped while checking out our options for getting to Venetie.

CHAPTER 10

Venetie

We chartered a direct flight from Fairbanks to Venetie for one hundred dollars with Don Garwood. The flight took a little over an hour in his Bonanza aircraft. I felt a strange apprehension about returning, but it was dispelled when we were greeted warmly at the airstrip by Abraham and Johnny's son Nathaniel, and the school teacher Mr. Birchell and his son David—and even Johnny.

Johnny was chief again. He and Sarah had come to Venetie for Christmas, and Johnny was persuaded to stay and help. He had been chief years before. It had not been a good experience, evidently, as he'd told me he'd never be chief again.

We went with Dick Birchell to visit his wife, Mildred, and their children. Then we walked over to speak to Johnny and Sarah, who were living with their son Hamel and his family in the community hall, a large log cabin.

"Where is Volk?" Johnny asked. "We never hear anything. He never send tobacco, too, like he say."

"He's in the Air Force and asked me to tell everyone hello for him."

Sarah served tea. We settled down to hear Johnny's stories. I had forgotten having some difficulty understanding Johnny the previous summer. Willy was attentive, and I had no idea that he was lost until, as a preface to a story, Johnny looked at him and asked, "You know Samson?"

"No," responded Willy.

I looked up. Johnny hesitated and then gave a synopsis of Samson's life—being a strong man, killing many men with a jawbone club, having his hair cut and losing his strength, blinded, and finally pushing down the temple columns. Everyone died. Samson's body was the only one not crushed. Then Johnny summarized the analogous Gwich'in story. Willy nodded now and then, appearing to take it all in.

Then, as Johnny began to tell the story about the Eskimo who came back to life, Johnny looked at Willy, "You know Jesus?"

"No," Willy replied again. This drew a prolonged silence. Johnny studied Willy as he filled his pipe. I knew Willy's mother—she would be appalled. She had raised him in the Southern Baptist Church from childhood and was deeply involved in church work. It was hard to keep from laughing. Willy was going to hear the long version.

Johnny outlined the life of Jesus—"the best man," as he called him. After much detail, he finally told of Jesus's death on the cross, a thief on either side, one who accepted Jesus and the other who rejected him; the soldiers; the nails driven into Jesus's hands and feet; the spear wound in his side. Then Johnny abruptly changed the subject. He probably believes we need missionaries now, I thought.

Sarah and her daughter Maggie were tanning moose skins. One was nearly finished, already soft and beautiful, ready for smoking. They placed it around a conical frame made of willow and covered it with a tarp.

"We keep little smoldering smoke fire going for few days," Maggie explained. "We move skin around some to get even gold color. We already put a raw skin in tub to soak for three days. We put chips of Ivory soap in there to help loosen hair."

Sarah and Maggie sat on the floor and draped the raw skin over the well-smoothed end of a two-foot pole with the hair pointing down. Sarah drew a butcher knife downward, removing a strip of hair. The blade angle was critical so as not to cut the hide. It was slow, intense work.

Dick and Mildred Birchell kindly took us in. We slept on their living room floor in the large log house that was the teachers' quarters. Mildred prepared huge meals, which we heartily shared with the family. Fortunately they had a large supply of food, which they ordered in bulk. The Bureau of Indian Affairs school and teachers' quarters had the only electricity in Venetie, produced by a diesel generator that could be heard anywhere in the village—and beyond. Ted and I enjoyed telling the younger children ghost stories from our childhood as they sat spellbound.

Walking around Venetie with Dick Birchell we saw changes. The cabins, school, and gardens were on a level area near the Chandalar River, backed by a cut bank thirty to forty feet high. The summer before everyone had individual gardens in their yards. Now families had plots in a large common area, which made watering easier. The plants were a foot high and well tended. Dick had acquired a portable water pump and organized an irrigation schedule, running an old fire hose from the river. He and David had built a greenhouse of heavy plastic sheeting over a frame. Inside, corn and tomatoes were flourishing forty miles north of the Arctic Circle. They grew lettuce and other vegetables, too, and Dick encouraged the villagers to expand their gardens beyond potatoes.

A new school was going up. The large frame building seemed out of place among the small log cabins. Most of the labor was hired in the village. There was no scarcity of food this year as every available male had a job paying two dollars and fifty cents an hour.

Johnny had snares and traps out and was catching rabbits and ground squirrels regularly. "Not many people do this now," he said.

We met Clara John out setting her little trap line. She was a teaching aide at the school. Her sister, Jessie, was the community health aide. Both had graduated from high school at Mt. Edgecombe, the BIA school in Sitka, the first from Venetie to do so.

I talked with Johnny about going to Gold Camp and Ackerman Lake. He wanted to go to Gold Camp but wasn't ready. In the meantime Ted, Willy, David Birchell, and I decided to cut and split firewood for sale at the going rate of thirty dollars a cord—a stack four feet high by eight feet long and four feet deep. Johnny approved.

People wanted dry wood. The closest stand of dead trees was several miles upriver and a quarter-mile inland. We borrowed a bow saw and axes. There were no chainsaws or motorized vehicles in Venetie in 1962, other than a few outboard motors for boats. We cut trees, hauled them to the river, and made a raft. David Birchell and I took the first raft down, trying to stay clear of the shallows. Once in a while we ran aground and had to struggle to free the raft. We took a swim on the way downriver. The water was so shockingly cold it took your breath away.

At the edge of the village we dismantled the raft, allowed the wood to dry overnight, and then sawed it into two-foot lengths. To move the wood we borrowed an old wheelbarrow with an iron wheel that wobbled loosely on the axle. Cut and stacked, the contents of our first raft amounted to about two-thirds of a cord. With the four of us working, it took one hour to cut enough trees for a raft and three hours to carry them to the river. Our total for a week's work was one hundred twenty dollars—four cords at thirty dollars each.

On Sunday, July 1, we rested, washed, and read. Johnny invited us to dinner, which included moose-head soup, a local delicacy made from cubes of meat carefully cut from the head. The soup was excellent. The nose of the moose, cut into chunks and boiled, made a very chewy side dish. I resisted laughing at Willy as he looked at the moose nose. David Salmon, an Episcopal minister and Gwich'in spiritual leader from Chalkyitsik, ate with us. As we sat and talked, villagers drifted in, helped themselves, and left, often without speaking.

On Monday we finished woodcutting. David and Ted were bringing down the last raft. Willy and I were on foot, carrying the tools, when a runner came with a note from the village health aide.

"Come quick," it said. "A little girl is having a seizure."

The village had chosen Jessie John to be their health aide; she was practical and responsible but had little formal training. We both had some hands-on experience, mine in medical school and accompanying my father on house calls and responding to emergencies.

The messenger led us to Joe Druck's cabin, which was packed with people. More spilled out the door into the yard. I anxiously pushed my way to the bed. Jessie was nowhere in sight. I cleared the mob from the cabin. Two women held a four-year-old girl, Becky, who was shaking violently. They held a stick in her mouth to keep her from chewing her tongue. After calming myself and the child, I removed the stick. Her respiration and pulse returned to normal but at intervals she shook uncontrollably. Becky had gotten into her grandmother's medicine and drunk a bottle of Benadryl, an allergy medicine.

Jessie appeared. She had made a radio call and a medivac was on the way. We held Becky and talked to her until a plane and nurse arrived and flew her to the hospital in Tanana on the Yukon River below Fort Yukon. I was relieved to see her go. Becky recovered and returned to Venetie in a few days.

In the evenings we stopped at Clara's coffee shop. This was a gathering place for the young people, many of whom attended the Chemawa Indian School in Salem, Oregon, where they learned popular dances. Clara's was the only place in Venetie to dance. Loud music played there on battery power, including such songs as Cotton Fields—"when them cotton bolls get rotten." One evening I talked Johnny into going. We sat for a few minutes before he announced that Clara's was not a place for him and left shaking his head.

We were still in Venetie on the Fourth of July. I was impatient to leave but Sarah and Maggie asked us to wait. I did not know what an important holiday this was in the village.

Some of the men had gone upriver hunting and brought home a moose for a potlatch at Johnny and Sarah's. The whole village turned out, more than one hundred people. Children were dressed in new clothes. Families brought plates and utensils. Fried meat, boiled meat, bannock bread, biscuits, tea, and other offerings filled the table. The moose was tender and tasty. There was plenty for all.

Later, the games began at the air strip. First were foot races, grouped by age. Contestants went all out. Girls won most of the races. For those over twelve, the races were by gender. Vera Erick won the women's race. People insisted we compete though we preferred to be spectators. I came in second in the men's race, easily outdistanced by Neil Sam, who ran in moccasins. David Birchell was third. We placed in the same order running backward. Ted entered the sack race. After the men's and women's nail-pounding contest, Joe Druck and Walter John chose sides for a tug of war with Ted and Willy joining Joe's team and me joining Walter's. This spirited event brought loud encouragement from everyone. Walter's team won.

Then the wrestling began. I was asked to referee. The matches were vigorous and serious as small kids struggled and rolled in the dirt in their new clothes. A good-natured attitude prevailed but the competition was stiff.

The pole-climbing event took place in front of the community cabin, where contestants worked their way up a spruce flagpole about thirty feet high. Some just wouldn't give up trying to get to the top. David Birchell climbed halfway up, higher than anyone else, on his fourth or fifth try. Trees were much taller where I grew up, and I liked high places. Ted or Willy told the Birchells and several others that I could climb. Urged on, I had no trouble climbing up and was nearing the top when Dick warned me that the pole was wobbling.

My climbing surprised them. Many people came by to shake my hand, including Ginnis Golan, whose cabin Abraham Christian had loaned us the previous summer. Ginnis was perhaps five feet tall and wore an old-style Canadian Stetson with a peaked top that sat comfortably on his head. These hats were common in the early days but now he and Johnny were the only men we saw wearing them.

"By golly, I never see that before!" Ginnis exclaimed, grinning widely, and pressed a silver dollar into my hand. The next day, Jimmy John, Sarah's brother, came over to me while I was sawing wood and gave me another silver dollar.

Jenny Sam, who appeared to be in her fifties, introduced herself and proclaimed Ted and me to be her brothers. The following day I was touched when she gave me a beautifully beaded velveteen tobacco pouch. Years later I learned that her brother Mike had drowned and that I was the first Mike she'd met since his death. Thereafter she always called me her brother.

Stephen Fredson invited me to his home for lunch where I shared fried moose and drank tea with him and his wife. Stephen seemed tense and his hands shook.

"In World War II, I was a soldier in the Aleutian Islands for nearly two years," he explained. "The Japanese invaded Alaska there and we fought them. Ever since I'm nervous ... like this."

Willy helped Mr. Birchell pull targets for a rifle match, the final competition. Around ten that evening, Willy and I went to a dance at the new school. It was well underway with the sounds of fiddle and guitar music spilling out into the summer evening. The place was packed and small groups stood outside the door. We squeezed inside, edging along a wall, listening to David Salmon play fiddle and Stanley Frank guitar. "Eight couple" dancing was followed by a single jig in which couples dance one at a time. Clara John dragged me out onto the floor where I felt conspicuous.

Square dances, rabbit and duck dances, and more eight-couple followed. There were many excellent dancers here. Someone was always pulling Willy and me into a dance, much to the amusement of the crowd. Vera Erick came over frequently, asking, "Mike, you be my partner?" At the end of each dance, couples went outside for fresh air and a smoke. Many of the children smoked, too. Noah Peter relieved David on the fiddle. When Ted arrived late, Clara immediately grabbed him, and he danced until the music ended around three in the morning.

I spent the next morning visiting with Jimmy John, a quiet, gentle elder. He lived in Arctic Village but had come to Venetie for the summer to garden, living in a tent overlooking the village and river. He told several bear stories.

In the evening I bathed in the Birchell's tub, a fifty-five-gallon oil drum cut in half and placed in the kitchen. We heated water on the stove. It felt good to soak. Afterward, I went to see Johnny, but I had no luck persuading him to leave the next morning.

Pulling out a bundle of letters, Johnny said, "Read these," and passed them to me. "I need to write letters before we go."

Johnny was noncommittal as to when he would be ready to head upriver, but we decided Willy, Ted, and David Birchell would leave the next morning. If Johnny was not ready by that evening, I'd go alone. Dick Birchell had asked me to take David, believing it would be good for his oldest son to go with us and come under my discipline. I guess my years at a military college showed. David was big for fourteen and was about my size, five-foot-seven and 145 pounds. He was strong and capable but had reached the age where he knew everything and was resistant to parental guidance. Dick realized that David's presence would have an effect on the harmony of our threesome. I could not refuse his request.

Ted, Willie, and David left at seven in the morning on July 6. David said he knew how to get to Gold Camp, having visited several times in the winter. Ted admitted he did not know the route. The day was clear and warm. There was virtually twenty-four hours of daylight that time of year.

Johnny had me write a letter objecting to a plan to dam the Yukon River at Rampart, which would flood many Gwich'in villages. We spent the rest of the morning going through papers describing requirements for federal rural development projects and wrote up grant proposals. One project would re-establish a route for whitefish to get into Big Lake from a creek that flowed into the Chandalar River. Years before there had been a natural connection allowing the netting of many whitefish, an important source of food. Local opinion was that a ditch would bring back this resource. Another proposal was for assistance building cabins with grant money going for labor and materials such as windows and roofing. At first I was alarmed at the need to supply the full names, ages, dependents' names, and Social Security numbers for all who would be involved but this went surprisingly well. I got all of the information together for the twenty-six prospective workers.

Jessie John gave me a bag of beans and a box of Jell-O for the trip and a beaded bracelet for my sister Barbara. Her generosity overwhelmed me. Back and forth I went to Johnny's. Finally Clara and Maggie told me he was ready to pack and that there was room in the dog packs for some of my gear. I brought over my deerskin jacket, a Christmas gift from my parents, and some food. The women sorted and packed. We would take four of Johnny's dogs. Three of them—*Vat'aii*, Leader, and Granger—would carry packs, their weights ranging from eighteen to twenty-seven pounds. Blackie would go without a pack, as only three were available.

My pack weighed about forty pounds, not including my rifle, pistol and a canteen of water. Johnny, then eighty-two, packed about fifteen pounds and carried his Model 95 Winchester. We finally left at half past six. Dick Birchell took pictures of our departure.

At Big Lake we went the long way around the east side, where the ground was dry. There was more water in the lake this year. We rejoined the trail on the other side and stopped to make tea. When the sun went behind the mountain, I opened the dog packs but did not find my jacket. Johnny's head net was missing, too. From there we climbed steadily. Johnny's leg cramped the first six or seven miles on the way to *Natl'at Van*, Cranberry Lake, where we found a partially burned sock. Ted, Willy, and David must have taken the shorter but wetter route around Big Lake and stopped to dry off. We walked several more miles before stopping on the mountainside. Johnny set snares while I cooked rice to go with our tea and dry caribou meat from Arctic Village. We slept a few hours.

Later, as we crossed Brush Mountain, an airplane flew over toward Gold Camp and returned a short while later. We were surprised. We'd hoped to avoid the thirty-six-mile walk, but when Johnny asked Keith Harrington, the Wien pilot, to fly us, Keith refused. "Johnny," he said, "clean up that strip first, then I'll land there. It might be pretty bad. Nobody has been there since breakup."

We walked down past the two little moose lakes and up the steep trail of Rock Mountain. On top we had tea, dry meat, and mush, and then dozed in the sun, leaning against our packs. The mosquitoes grew progressively worse as we went along, even on the ridge top, because there was no breeze to blow them away. The brush was about mid-calf to knee-high. Even wearing my head net the buzzing was an irritation. Not usually social, the dogs would approach, noses totally covered with mosquitoes, which I crushed and brushed away with my gloved hand. At other times the dogs would walk off the faint trail, rubbing their noses against the brush. Johnny applied Off mosquito repellent liberally but it seemed to be of little help.

"Off no goddamn good! Like water," Johnny exclaimed, the only time I ever heard him cuss.

This went on for miles. Every fifteen to twenty minutes we stopped to make a small fire onto which we threw handfuls of a low-growing plant that made a lot of smoke, driving back the bugs. I remembered that the previous year our record for mosquitoes killed with a single swat by one hand was eighteen, an honor held by Ted. This year my numbers climbed steadily. I swatted 28, 42, and finally 63!

As I fed a smoke fire, I noticed a green spot in the lichen, a bright color that looked so out of place I took off my glove and touched it. It was wet paint. I turned to Johnny, baffled. This made no sense to me.

"Where you get that?" Johnny asked anxiously. "Take off the dog packs! Paint!"

When I slipped my hand behind Granger's pack it was wet and sticky. For some while his pack had been sliding back and his leg knocking against something metal inside. Finally, the dog would come up to me and I'd pull his pack back up onto his shoulders, which helped until the next time.

"The paint is for canvas boat, waterproof," Johnny said. As we unpacked, we found the leaking can. Tightly rolled into a ball and stuffed into several flour sacks was my jacket, now decorated with green paint that had soaked through the sacks. Still, I was glad to find it and put it on. We also found Johnny's head net.

As we went on, Leader began to fall behind, and we stopped several times to wait for him. Leader had the heaviest pack. This was the first trip of the year for the dogs. By then it was drizzling but Johnny's spirits were high. So were Leader's after I relieved him of a ten-pound bag of sugar.

At one point we saw a huge set of trophy-sized moose antlers hanging in a small spruce. I'd never seen such antlers and stood staring.

"Big bull moose, by golly, really big one!" Johnny exclaimed.

Finally we could see the East Fork from the ridge top and started down the mountain. A good trail wound through a spruce forest for the last four or five miles to the river.

After a meal of boiled dry meat and rice, bannock bread, and tea, I scanned the valley looking for signs of the others but saw nothing. We'd not seen any trace of them for quite a while and I was starting to worry that they might be lost. The route across the ridge tops was faint.

"Nobody walk to Gold Camp much anymore. Brush is getting big, too," Johnny said.

The next morning I found Ted and the others camped upriver. Ted had just returned from Gold Camp where he'd spent a miserable night. They had gotten lost, having come down off the ridge too soon, and spent half a day fighting their way through thick willows and alders. When they arrived opposite Gold Camp, they saw smoke from the cabin. Ted undressed and swam the main channel. In the small cabin he found Robert Frank, one of Johnny's grandsons, and Jonathan Tritt, both twenty. They did not invite him in even though he stood shaking cold and wet in his underwear.

Robert told Ted that both boats were gone, probably washed away in the high water at breakup, and that a bear had broken into the new cabin.

The cabin we had built the previous summer was a complete mess. The door was broken in. Ted found some long underwear and old moccasins and put them on to fight off the mosquitoes and cold. Snow had drifted into the cabin over the winter and melted with the arrival of summer. Large sacks of rice, beans, and flour had been broken into and now lay mildewed about the cabin. The stench was awful. Ted intended to spend the night there but he had no matches. After a few miserable hours he swam back across the river with an ax and rope to make a raft. I was impressed. The current was swift and icy cold.

I went downstream to get Johnny, and we brought our gear and the dogs to their camp. About then Jonathan and Robert appeared on the opposite riverbank. Johnny yelled instructions to them. "My canvas boat is downriver at the slough. Bring it."

A couple hours later they returned without finding the boat. So Johnny started cutting down dead trees and we hauled them to the river. Finally, we had enough logs to make a raft to carry two people and all the gear. Ted and Johnny took the packs and our clothes across, fighting the fast-moving current. Willy, David, and I swam, as did the dogs. On the other side, Willy asked for his glasses as we dressed. He'd handed them over to Ted for safekeeping.

Ted reached for his pocket, "Willy, I lost them!" Willy had very poor vision and had no second pair. We searched up and down the bank. Ted swam back across the river and returned. No glasses.

Johnny and Sarah had left Gold Camp in December expecting to return in a week or two. But now it had been six months. He looked at the broken door and two smashed windows. Spoiled food and wet, moldy blankets and clothing lay scattered about. Caribou hides were rotting. It was a disaster. Johnny sorted everything to decide what was salvageable, occasionally shaking his head and looking serious but overall taking it in stride. On the walk over, he'd said, "Well, I try one more time to be chief but no use. Nobody listen. Last time for me. I'll just stay here." Johnny figured that if he and Sarah had returned to Gold Camp as planned, none of this would have happened.

We went back to the little cabin. Johnny left to set snares. He set six and the next morning returned with five rabbits and a ground squirrel. Robert and Jonathan hunted moose. Willy and I hunted eyeglasses. As we sat around the fire, Willy had told us he could not see beyond about six or eight feet without them. After scouring the riverbank once again, we finally gave up, deciding they must have fallen into the river. Then, without looking, I happen to find the eyeglasses squashed into the mud and grass in a stand of trees. Ted had been there retrieving the long underwear he'd left hanging in a tree. We were elated to find them unbroken.

FOR SEVERAL DAYS we cleaned the cabins and surrounding area, set snares, caught rabbits, and fished for grayling. Robert and Jonathan hunted without success. In the evenings we played cards. The weather remained cloudy and rainy.

On the way over, all had not been congenial with the advance party. Not only did David Birchell not know the way to Gold Camp but he'd also refused to help gather wood or water, cook, or wash dishes. I took steps to correct this. My approach was abrupt—"It's your turn, wash the dishes!" I demanded. Slowly David became more responsive until eventually he took his turns spontaneously, and our morale improved.

The Wien pilot had found the landing strip to be satisfactory, but we worked to improve it anyway. We were waiting for him to deliver Sarah, Maggie, and Clara. When the plane did not arrive, Johnny decided against going to Ackerman Lake. Robert and Jonathan had no luck hunting and vacillated about whether to go with us. Jonathan had never been to the lake and Robert had been there when so young that his father had packed him in on his back.

The weather was clear but still no airplane. Blackie got loose and ruined four rabbits in Johnny's snares. We were packed and ready to go when Robert and Jonathan decided to come. Johnny told them they could take Blackie as a pack dog; he would wait for the plane and hunt. We made good time to Six Mile Fork and on to *Git tsal*. Our meager supplies diminished quickly with six of us. Our feet were sore and our pace slowed. Robert's only footwear was a pair of military dress shoes. Robert was friendly and smiled a lot, never complaining or mentioning his poor footwear. Jonathan was quiet and stone-faced but was a good companion. Willy looked tired but never complained and always did his share of the work. David was strong, hiked well, and was boastful. But he was young so we figured he had a good chance of outgrowing his attitude.

The weather turned cloudy and drizzly. I explained that Johnny's trail went in a round-about manner and that we'd discovered a more direct route coming back from Ackerman to *Git tsal*. We took the direct route, a mistake. Crossing the creek, we saw our mountaintop objective in the distance across a broad valley. All day we pushed through thick willows without a trail. I led. Most of the time we walked in water and the rain soaked the rest of us. We came across a little rise with two spruce trees. The ground was relatively dry beneath them so we took a break. I was amazed to see Jonathan extract dry cigarettes for a smoke.

All afternoon we slogged on. I parted the ever-thick willows with my rifle barrel. No one spoke. I was beyond tired, becoming exhausted, but there was no place to rest. Still I would not give up the lead. Suddenly I was looking down, as if in a dream, from far above and a little behind us. I saw all of us, including myself, crossing a great expanse single file. This vision lasted a few minutes. Later I realized this had been an out-of-body experience. But at the time I was too tired to care.

Finally, we arrived at the foot of the mountain, *Neeteiindrat,* and stopped to build a fire in a small stand of dead trees. Jonathan threw off his pack. We gathered wood. By then I was shaking uncontrollably. There were no dry spruce twigs for kindling, so Jonathan got a fire going by shaking his bottle of Off, which is flammable, onto the wood. This was no place to camp but we were reluctant to leave after drying off and getting warm.

We headed slowly up the mountain. I pushed on until out of breath, then paused and rested while standing. Near the top we stopped to graze on ripe cranberries. Jonathan killed a porcupine, which Robert carried as he had only tea, mush, and sugar in his pack. From the summit we looked down on both lakes and spotted the cabins. It seemed a long way yet, but we moved downhill at a good pace. I found the key and unlocked the cabin. The stack of dry wood and kindling we'd cut the year before was a welcome sight. Soon a fire blazed in the stove. By then it was three or four in the morning. As soon as we were dry and shared coffee we fell asleep.

I awoke to the smell of burning hair. Jonathan was burning the hair and quills off the porcupine over a small fire in front of the cabin. He scraped the burned remains with a stick. Then he gutted the porcupine and cut it up to boil. We fished but had no success at first. Finally Willy and Ted caught a seventeen-inch pike. We ate the porcupine and began to prepare the fish. Jonathan and Robert had mentioned earlier that they might go on to the Middle Fork, west of Ackerman Lake, to hunt and look for wolf dens. Around midnight they packed their gear, readied Blackie, and left without a word.

We straightened up the cabin and played cards, enjoying cooked apples on bannock bread with milk and sugar. We made Canadian tea, which grew everywhere. Our group was now quite compatible. David was even learning to say "please" and "thank you!"

Our energy levels were low and we felt lazy and nonproductive. We fished, ate, gathered wood, trapped, and played cribbage. Willy caught a few lake trout. At a nearby pond I shot a duck with the .22. It got off the water and flew straight at me, expiring right at the shoreline. In the distance I heard Willy shout to Ted, "I found the pike. Come over here!"

After plucking and cleaning the duck I found them fishing from a long rocky point where the water was shallow and clear. The pike moved with ease among the reed grass. Ted caught five pike and, at his urging, I caught several.

Ted and I cleaned the fish while David got a fire ready. We prepared a banquet: duck soup, mashed potatoes, bannock, and half a broiled pike for each of us. The meat was firm and white. The numerous thin bones did not bother us. We ate stewed apples on bannock for dessert.

The next day the pike were not interested in lures. At the cabin, I found a long fish spear made of a flared caribou rib with nail spikes. I waded in the water among the reeds looking for pike in the shallows. Several times I struck and grazed a pike, once scarring a big one's side. All the large pike we caught had healed battle scars. With a good frog jig I could have gotten fish, I thought. The bone flares had to be turned just so and slowed movement through the water. Still, it was a feasible if difficult method to catch pike. No wonder the

Gwich'in spent most of their time in the old days working to procure food.

Sarah spoke of those times with respect for the tenacity of survivors. There were many stories of hardship, extreme courage, and intermittent times of starvation. I thought back to a story she told and her daughter Maggie translated.

Once, when there had been no animals or food, a small band of hunters came across fresh moose tracks leading to a little island of willows and spruce. No tracks led out. Waist-deep snow lay on the river ice and it was cold, maybe forty below. At this temperature, dry snow crunches loudly underfoot. This noise and that of caribou pants brushing the snow would alarm the moose. The men decided one of them would approach downwind; he would need to get very close in order to kill the moose with a bow and arrow. The arrow point was bone or antler, sharpened to the fine point necessary to penetrate the thick skin deeply enough to be fatal or, at least, to wound the animal severely. The hunters' situation was desperate. Their children were weak with hunger. Dogs had starved.

"My grandfather take off parka and skin pants little way from island—just wear skin boots," Sarah related. "He went slowly onto the island breaking a new path. The moose would run if followed on its own trail. He killed the moose. Lots of people saved that way. Hard time but no sickness then, just later after white man come. Hard time but people happy. Everybody work hard."

That summer of 1962 we had the advantage of technology, some store-bought food, and the relative ease of summer living. Still, we spent many hours catching fish, rabbits, ground squirrels, and ducks. From Venetie to Ackerman Lake, a distance of about seventy-five miles, we'd not seen one large animal, though frequently their tracks were fresh in the trail. Because there was an ever-present concern about not having enough to eat, we ate more than usual when we had it, wasting nothing.

WE BEGAN OUR return to Gold Camp by heading up the mountain. The top was tundra and firm ground. We looked over the entire countryside. No one else was here. The hills rolled away to the east and south. Beyond the lakes to the north rose mountain after mountain. I had not climbed *Ch'idrii*, Heart Mountain—maybe someday, I thought as I looked at it. The day was clear and sunny. A light breeze kept the mosquitoes away. I could not stop gazing at this vast, wild country so different from my home in South Carolina. I loved being in this place where I felt a sense of freedom and deep satisfaction.

From the height we looked ahead to choose our route carefully, determined not to relive the difficulty of our hike in. The dark, slender lines among the lighter green would be spruce trees. I sought the best linkage of them across the expanse. *Git tsal* was about twenty-five miles from the cabins. We had come perhaps three miles. Though reluctant to depart this idyllic spot, we headed down the mountain, traversing a series of small, bare hills separated at regular intervals by drainages of water thick with willows. Walking here was unexpectedly good, and drinking water was plentiful.

I was leading when I heard a cry. I thought someone had slipped and fallen into the water, which would be cold but not dangerous. I walked on a way before stopping to wait. As the others caught up, someone stumbled into me, and I turned to chastise him. Ted stood wavering with his hand over one eye, tears on his face.

"Sorry," he said. "I stuck a stick in my eye when I leaned over to get water."

There was a large, rough cut radiating out across the cornea of his right eye. I knew it had to be quite painful. Already Ted had a headache and was feeling dizzy.

"Are you able to keep going?" I asked.

"Yeah. It's hard to judge distance, though. I might go slower."

We waded the creek and went on to *Git tsal*, where we camped. I re-examined Ted, applied salve from the first-aid kit, and bandaged his eye. David and Willy returned with grayling, which we boiled vertically, head or tail first in a coffee can. These we ate head, bones, and all. Willy had gotten wet in the creek and tried to dry his boots as we huddled near the fire. With the sun obscured, there was a definite chill in the air and it was starting to get darker at "night." I reached for a canteen and found it partially frozen.

The next day we found the previous year's bear camp. Nearby in one of Johnny's snares was a rotted caribou. Half way to Six Mile Fork we came across a tent Johnny had pitched in our absence. Johnny had been hunting here. It was the six-by-eight-foot canvas wall tent. Though small, it was still bulky and heavy. I visualized him making several trips to this place fourteen miles or so from Gold Camp, including one thigh-deep stream crossing in swift, cold water. Even with the dogs it would be arduous at his age.

We stopped several times to make tea or rest. It was a long day, difficult for Ted but he kept up, never complaining. The injury still hurt but he was no longer dizzy.

Johnny was alone at Gold Camp. We had been away for six days. The plane had not come. Johnny cooked grayling and bannock bread for us.

"Nobody come," he said. "I hunt every day. I never even see one moose. You see my tent? You look inside?"

"No, but David did," I replied.

"You take something?" he asked David. "I left snares, grub, poncho, tobacco."

"Yes, a poncho," David said, to my surprise. He returned it to Johnny.

"No snares?" Johnny asked him.

"Nothing else."

Johnny had cleaned the new cabin but it still had the mildew smell. "Sometime I'll move it up on the hill, use those logs," he said. "Better there." It was a bit swampy around the cabin and did not have a good view across the river.

Johnny had continued to catch rabbits, grayling, and ground squirrels. That morning he showed us seven large rabbits. After breakfast he returned from his main cache, which was set some fifteen feet above the ground and reachable only by ladder. He was displeased.

"Somebody take raisins from cache," he said. "I saw David go that way. Big box raisins."

"Did you take raisins from the cache, David?" I asked.

"Yes," he admitted, "I ate them."

"No good to steal," Johnny admonished. "You need it, I give it to you. Don't steal."

David apologized and helped Johnny and me put canvas on a new canoe frame Johnny made while we were gone.

"You have been a busy man, Johnny!"

"Yes, never stop, just keep on, all my life!" he smiled. "Now I can take you across river."

"What will you do? Go with us?"

"No. I wait on Robert. He borrow my boots, so I only got these rubber boots," he said, indicating his bulky knee-high rubber boots. "No good for walking long way."

I didn't mention that Robert had worn his army shoes on the hike to Ackerman Lake and beyond. I had not seen Johnny's boots.

We left Gold Camp the next day, July 18, carrying our packs and the canoe across the gravel bars and shallow streams to the main channel. To increase stability and flotation, we fastened a dry log to either side of the small craft. Johnny ferried us across the river one at a time. The boat drifted quite a way downriver in the rapid current and each time we brought it back up for another crossing.

Once we were all across, Johnny removed his treasured Canadian Stetson, a peaked-crown, flat-brimmed hat popular years before. It is still worn by the Royal Canadian Mounted Police and Marine Corps drill instructors. It was very practical, keeping rain off the head and neck and brush out of the eye. The wide brim kept a mosquito head net away from the face. Johnny knew that I admired his Stetson.

"You take it," he said, handing it to me.

I hesitated, wanting the hat but reluctant.

He smiled, "You take it."

The hat fit well. I felt deeply moved.

"I buy it from Japanese Frank at Beaver, maybe 1942. He got a store that time. Good man, too! You keep it. You remember for me."

We removed the logs from the canoe and watched him cross back alone. Then we headed up the trail. Halfway to Venetie we slept for a few hours on the tundra and then went on. Ted was able to hike the last ten miles without an eye patch.

"How's your eye?" I asked.

"Better. Not much pain now but I still see double."

We stopped at *Natl'at Van*. There were no ducks or lynx this time. From here the trail was good and pleasantly downhill to the shore of Big Lake, *Van Choo*. We took the short route around Big Lake. The water was mostly knee deep, occasionally rising to the upper thigh, for two-thirds of a mile. There we met Clara, Jenny, and Eddie John with the Rev. Don Nelson, the KJNP missionary. They were also headed for Venetie, but had stopped to look for Don's sunglasses, lost the day before. Clara wanted to take my pack or rifle but I resisted. Ted was glad to give up his rifle.

At Venetie, we were alarmed to find Robert and Jonathan, who had returned to the village by raft, losing Blackie in the process. They had killed a moose but left most of it behind.

"You know Johnny is waiting for you," I said. "Why didn't you go back to Gold Camp?"

I was angry, thinking of Johnny awaiting the return of his boots and his favorite dog. Robert just grinned and looked at the ground. He didn't respond.

We stayed with the Birchells again. Dick thought the trip had been good for David and I had to agree. David was strong and resourceful. In spite of our friction early on, he'd been a fine hiker, did not complain, and responded well to guidance. I understood that mid-teen years are difficult.

We helped around the house, weeded in the garden, and worked with Dick, who was building a riverboat. He was waiting for an outboard motor he'd ordered. We were glad to change boots for soft beaded moccasins. We visited Sarah. She was concerned about Johnny. So was I. He was eighty-two, alone, and had only rubber boots. It was not an easy hike from Gold Camp to Venetie, even with three pack dogs.

We were welcomed at Clara's coffee shop. The loud, popular music was such a contrast to our summer in the wilderness. We were pressed to dance again, this time the Shag and the Twist, the newest dances learned at boarding school. We visited about the village—Abraham and Annie; Jessie and Clara; and the Frank, Sam, and Fredson families. We heard many good stories.

Johnny arrived on foot before we left Venetie. He was in good health but unhappy to learn that Blackie was lost. Later we learned from a letter that Jonathan and Robert had gone back upriver by boat to retrieve the moose meat and look for Blackie. Johnny's dog had appeared on the riverbank, attracted by the sound of the outboard, hungry but otherwise unharmed.

CHAPTER 11

Leaving the South

Five years passed before I returned to Alaska in January 1967. I enjoyed the clinical work my last two years of medical school and stuck it out to graduate in June 1964. To my surprise, I came to dislike general surgery, the specialty I'd expected to pursue. The four- to five-year residency was part of an autocratic, rigid class system. I'd had enough of this at The Citadel. Residents spent long hours evaluating, operating on, and caring for patients while subservient to the whims of the attending surgeons or a senior resident.

Surgery lasted hours in complicated cancer involvement and was often mutilating. Tubes dangled everywhere with fluids going in or out. In the operating room, anger made a frequent appearance as an upper-level resident openly belittled someone only a year behind. Interns were low in the pecking order. Students generally received a little better treatment.

My decision to find a new surgical specialty came during a twelve-hour "Whipple" procedure for cancer of the pancreas. The chief resident, Doctor Cook, was a mean, narrow-eyed man who had authority but little respect. Three residents and I were scrubbed in with Doctor Cook as surgeon. My job was to retract the liver. The surgeon's communication to me was a clang on the retractor with scissors or needle holder and an occasional verbal demand to pull harder. I responded, trying not to tear the liver. Doctor Cook ridiculed an excellent fourth-year resident. The procedure was extensive—a radical removal of part of the pancreas, stomach, and intestine. Sometimes it succeeded.

I asked permission to leave the operating room to attend a lecture; as a medical student, I should have been allowed go. He ignored me. Seven or eight hours into the surgery, Doctor Cook told me to cut sutures, removing the extra material after he tied the knot. After repeatedly hearing "too long, too short" and seeing a variance of only one-sixteenth to one-eighth of an inch, I tossed the scissors onto the instrument tray.

He exploded, "Take the scissors!"

"Cut them yourself," I replied. "No one can please you."

I refused to take them. He picked up the scissors and struck me hard across the back of my hand, "Take these!" I refused without further comment. I was now on his list. Students did not talk back or rebel.

Fortunately the patient survived the surgery. Obtaining good results was possible in this atmosphere but I wanted none of it.

THE SUMMER BETWEEN my junior and senior years I worked in South Carolina as an extern at Greenwood Memorial Hospital, the job I had passed up the previous year. At Greenwood my experience was far different. There were no interns or residents, so frequently I was first assistant in surgery. The surgeons were experienced and courteous.

Driving to the hospital one morning my father asked, "What are your plans for specializing?"

I held my father in utmost respect. He was a country doctor, as had been his father and grandfather, and he also performed surgery. It was a privilege to work with him. From childhood on I'd often accompanied him on house calls and off-hour office visits. He never urged us to go into medicine. It had been my decision.

Now he surprised me with advice.

"Don't go into general practice," he said. "Find a specialty you like. In general practice some seventy-five percent of the patients can't be helped. They are neurotic or have symptoms related to the life situation in which they are trapped. You cannot change that. Even in a chosen specialty there will be much that you will not like but have to do."

I returned to medical school in Charleston and chose orthopedics for my senior elective. The rotation was for a month, but by the end of the first day I knew this would be my field. Here one fixed things, put broken bones back together, corrected deformities, improved function, and prevented disability.

The attending orthopedists and residents treated each other and patients with respect. I was welcomed as part of the team, delighted to have found a surgical specialty that I could pursue without reserve. It was a great relief, as only two months remained before graduation in early June.

I began a straight surgical internship at the University of Virginia Medical Center in

Charlottesville the first of July. Straight internships were new at that time. Most interns rotated spending equal time in obstetrics, pediatrics, internal medicine, and surgery. My rotations were all surgical: general, emergency, neurosurgery, urology, orthopedics, plastic, chest, and cardiovascular. The schedule was grueling, officially thirty-six hours on and twelve hours off. In reality it was more like thirty-eight and ten. I needed a break. I was not ready to enter a residency program.

It was 1965. Letters from my Selective Service draft board arrived with increasing frequency. Most new doctors ended up in Vietnam. Only those enrolled in further training programs received deferments. Due to my military experience at The Citadel and my personal interest, I knew a lot about the political situation. Citadel graduates had already been in Southeast Asia, some clandestinely.

I read books on guerrilla warfare and everything I could find on Vietnam. A book by Major Paul Grauwin described his experience as the chief surgeon during the fifty-five-day siege of the French at Dien Bien Phu in 1954. This heroic but futile effort ended French colonialism in Vietnam. I supported Vietnamese independence and opposed U.S. involvement there.

Orders came to report for an Army physical. Young men filled the olive drab bus to Richmond. Naked, we stood in long lines waiting to be poked and prodded by military doctors. It was silent on the bus ride back to Charlottesville.

A few weeks later I took a day off to go to Washington, D.C. to inquire about a commission with the U.S. Public Health Service. This would fulfill my obligation to the Selective Service.

Before daylight I dripped ether from the emergency room into the carburetor on my old Plymouth before cranking the engine. It was bitterly cold. I could see the road through holes rusted in the floor but the car ran well and I had no problems. In Arlington, Virginia, I stopped for gas and a map to locate the PHS headquarters. Once there, I went from desk to desk seeking information on PHS surgical teams in Vietnam serving civilians.

"You have to have completed one year of a surgical residency to qualify as an assistant."

"I'm doing a new type of internship, straight surgical; it is equivalent."

"It is an internship. You don't qualify."

"Are there any other overseas programs?" I asked.

"Are you aware of our program with the Peace Corps?"

"No, but I'd be interested."

A month later, I was back in Washington for Peace Corps interviews. To qualify, I had to be accepted both as a commissioned officer in the PHS and by the Peace Corps' medical division. Once approved, frequent changes in my country assignment demonstrated disorganization in the administration of the program. Monthly I received a phone call informing me of a new assignment: Nepal, Sarawak, Kuala Lumpur, Nepal again, and finally Guatemala. The last call came during afternoon rounds in June on a day I had worked thirty-six hours straight and lost the struggle to keep a post-operative patient alive.

A doctor with the Peace Corps in Washington introduced himself on the phone, "I'm the medical director for Latin America."

"What do you want?" I asked briskly.

"What do you think of Guatemala?"

"Not a damn thing. Can't you people get organized?"

"Think about it and let me know. That is your assignment if you want to work with us."

The next day I accepted.

THE PEACE CORPS was not highly regarded in the conservative South. Typical was my experience at home before leaving. I sat in the barber chair where I had gotten haircuts most of my life. Four or five men sat waiting. In a gentle hum of low, unhurried voices, the conversation drifted—crops, weather, the cotton mill.

As he snipped away, Mr. Brock asked, "What are you up to now? I always get you and your two brothers mixed up."

"I just finished an internship in Virginia. I'm going to Guatemala."

Heads came up as attention turned our way. "One of my friends was there in World War II," one of the men offered.

"That was probably Guadalcanal. Guatemala is just south of Mexico."

"Why in the world are you going there?"

"To be a doctor in the Peace Corps," I said.

A sudden silence descended, then the subject was changed. "I hear the mill will be laying off this summer," somebody said.

My experience in the Peace Corps had a great impact on me. In 1954, the Central Intelligence Agency had backed a military coup against the duly elected government of Guatemala. This harsh dictatorship was still in power more than a decade later. The indigenous people, a majority of the population, lived under a virtual feudal system. I was outraged that our government supported the dictatorship with military and economic aid.

My job included visiting volunteers at their sites. Most volunteers in Guatemala worked in the nebulous field of community development with the goal of improving the lives of the local people. As Peace Corps workers adjusted to living in a foreign country, they went through a general pattern. The first month was exciting, being in a beautiful, exotic country, meeting people, and getting settled. By the third month depression often set in when many realized the odds of accomplishing our goal were remote. We scheduled a conference, bringing everyone together to share their experiences and frustration. Then, in the cycle of a volunteer's service, came a period of adapting expectations to reality. Those in structured assignments, such as teaching, had an easier time. By the end of the first year most volunteers had adapted to their situation and were more or less content during their remaining year.

I had come from a southern conservative background. Most volunteers came from a liberal one. Our long discussions opened me to reconsider my political views. Gradually I came to recognize the parallels of Guatemala's treatment of its indigenous peoples to the treatment of blacks in the South. I saw that having citizens with the experience of living in other countries was good for our own country.

After a year in Guatemala, I transferred to Santiago, Chile, as chief medical officer. Eduardo Frei, a Social Democrat, was president of this nation with its many political parties from far right to far left. Chileans were proud of their democracy and quick to point out their difference from other Latin American countries. Politics were openly debated there in contrast to Guatemala. Some eight hundred Peace Corps volunteers lived and worked throughout this long, narrow country, many of them in isolated areas.

One Friday afternoon I received a call from Kirk Breed, the Peace Corps' regional director for the Temuco area, about two hundred fifty miles south of Santiago. Kirk asked me to come down to evaluate the behavior of a volunteer who had come in from the nearby university city of Concepción with bizarre accusations directed at several other volunteers. I drove down that day. After listening to the volunteer for three hours, I knew he was on the verge of a mental breakdown and needed to be evacuated back to the states.

Kirk and I went to Concepción to talk with other volunteers, and that's where I met Elizabeth Neill. Kirk knocked on the door of a small house. Elizabeth opened the door, surprised to see us but self-assured and calm as Kirk explained our presence. She was an attractive brunette, a slim five-foot-six or so, and neatly dressed in a light turtleneck sweater and medium-length skirt.

Over the next few months we began dating and later traveled to Peru and Bolivia on vacation. On our return to Santiago I learned that Paul Bell, the new Peace Corps director for Chile, was upset with us.

"Paul wants to see you in his office on arrival. He is really pissed at you," said my colleague, Joe Segura.

"What is this about?"

"You and Liz going on vacation together."

"You are kidding!"

"No, and he isn't, either."

I went downstairs to Paul's office, finding it difficult to take this seriously. We'd not tried to hide our dating or our vacation together. In fact, a staff person had driven us to the Santiago airport to catch the flight to Lima.

"This is serious!" Paul Bell warned. Paul had been a Baptist missionary for five years in Central America. "Staff members are not to date volunteers. Sargent Shriver was lax about this but the new Peace Corps director, Jack Vaughn, is not. Jack sent out a memo reaffirming that staff cannot date volunteers. This is cause for dismissal unless you and Liz plan to marry."

"We have not discussed marriage."

"Well, if you are engaged, it's a different matter. If not, you are not to see her again."

"I'm not going to have that pressure on our relationship," I responded angrily, having no intention to comply.

Even though Elizabeth and I decided to marry, Paul sent us to Washington. At Peace Corps headquarters I received a two-page memo describing my moral transgression, insubordination, and willful disobedience of orders. I was stunned. My options were limited—resign or be fired.

Still a commissioned officer in the Public Health Service, I went to the Indian Health Service headquarters and inquired about positions in Alaska. I accepted a job at the regional hospital in the village of Kanakanak near Dillingham in southwest Alaska, about four hundred miles from Anchorage.

The next day I resigned from the Peace Corps.

SNOW SWIRLED THICKLY in the bright lights as Elizabeth and I carefully descended the stairs from the jet into a January blizzard that enveloped Anchorage. The wind whipped our faces. We pulled up the hoods of our new down parkas and walked quickly toward the terminal. All was dark beyond a circle of bright lights. I was acutely aware how alien this was for Elizabeth. Barely a month before, we were enjoying the pleasant Chilean summer. Now we found ourselves in the depth of a subarctic winter at the start of a new year, 1967.

We spent a few days in Anchorage for orientation at the Alaska Native Medical Center. I was surprised to learn that Maggie Roberts was a patient with resistant tuberculosis. TB had hit her family hard, as it had the entire Native population. Maggie said her parents were well. Johnny and Sarah still lived at Gold Camp. Several of her children were with them now.

THE KANAKANAK HOSPITAL complex was six miles from Dillingham, a fishing town on Bristol Bay. We lived in an aging four-plex in a government compound.

Most of the population in the eighteen villages around Bristol Bay was Aleut and Yupik Eskimo. Russian and Scandinavian names were common. Many families had surnames such as Cowboy or Snowball, given them by insensitive government clerks who could not, or would not, try to deal with Native names. In addition to our work at the clinic and hospital, we traveled twice a year to each village. The other docs did not like making these trips. I welcomed them, so I traveled a lot.

The medical work was interesting and varied. We handled most patients' problems ourselves, consulting by telephone with specialists at the medical center in Anchorage. We talked daily by radio with health aides in the villages, suggesting treatments or deciding to bring someone to the regional hospital when necessary. There was no such thing as medical privacy because our radio frequency was the same one used by the fishing fleet, and many people had radios in their homes.

In the spring I visited villages on the Alaska Peninsula in a light plane, taking my shotgun with me. Waterfowl were returning to nest—flocks of geese, ducks, sandhill cranes, and shorebirds added a sudden burst of life to the land. Natives looked forward to their return even though spring hunts were illegal. The desire for fresh meat, in short supply during the long winter, and strong cultural tradition overrode the federal restriction on hunting except in the fall. We flew over Herendeen Bay with tens of thousands of emperor geese below us.

Elizabeth, by then pregnant, worked in medical records. She spoke to me during the daily hospital radio call. "Have you gotten any geese yet?"

"It is not hunting season."

"There is a lot of static. I asked if you got any geese yet."

"No, it is not the season to hunt geese."

Of course our radio conversation had been heard far and wide. For the remainder of the trip, wherever I went into a village, someone teased me, "Doc, did you get any geese yet?" My shotgun remained packed.

CHAPTER 12

Back to Gwich'in Country

In mid-May, Elizabeth and I chartered a flight to Gold Camp. Johnny and Sarah seemed well. The weather was wonderful—springtime in interior Alaska. The snow was gone, the days were long and warm, and there were no bugs yet. Maggie and several of her children were there. I brought a tape recorder and showed them how it captured voices, explaining how I could send their message to Ted.

Johnny sat quietly for a little while, chewing his pipe stem, and then said, "Okay. Ready. You ready?" The children were hushed. Johnny leaned forward and spoke without hesitation, though he had never seen a recorder before.

"Well, hello Teddy. I want to see you this summer. You never come. I see you brother, you sister-in-law. We glad for everything. We talk 'em story, anything. Well, next time you get chance, you come up. I tell you lots story. You and me go hunt bear!" He laughed and Sarah chuckled. The children whispered in the background.

"You like grayling? Take easy up in river, on one side the bend, take easy all you want. One thing, no ground squirrels. In fall time lots of moose start running. About four miles upriver Lawrence kill three big bulls, one little place. I kill one, and my other grandchild, Hamel's son, Kenneth, kill too.

"That same place big bear come up every night. I set gun that night."

A set gun is difficult to use with accuracy. After a thorough study of the terrain, a loaded and

103

cocked gun is tied securely in place with a trip-string attached to the trigger. It was positioned to shoot the animal in a vital area with a single shot when it disturbs the trip-string.

"She shot 'em in own heart! Next morning I find big bear, dead," Johnny chuckled. "I cut off fat, lots of grease, all (over) my hands, my shirt. I quit my shirt. I quit my pants, too, all oil!"

Everyone laughed.

"Same time I find that bear, something come, take hair off, no break in skin. I think maybe no teeth. I set rifle again. Next day I go up, big black wolf right there, shot in neck," he laughs again. "Good story, eh?"

"Well, afterwards, little snow come. By golly! Millions of weasels all over, their tracks on the ground. Marten, the same. I set a few traps for weasels; I kill ten. One marten.

"I set a big trap, for wolf, number four got teeth.

"After a week I kill another big black wolf. We set it again, one red fox. Last time, cross fox. Next time I go up there, big white wolf, great one, 180 pounds! Fat all over. Eat lots animals, too much.

"After two weeks I go across the river to hunt on the big mountain. I kill big bull moose. I use trail snowshoes that time. Just me alone, I follow that moose. Big bull. I shot 'em. Next morning I go up with dog team. Three big dogs, strong. I bring back half. Well, that night wolverine come up. I see tracks there, set a trap in that wolverine track. Next morning, I go out again, big gray wolf. Next morning I go up last time. I bring a little meat, well, another wolverine.

"One thing, this fall I never see one caribou around Gold Camp. Other side, upriver, I never see one track. One thing, lots of marten, any place on river or up on mountain, anyplace! All gone now; I don't know where. Well, when you stay here that time used to be lots of rabbits, you remember? Lots of rabbits up on the bank? I never see one track now. Nothing. No ground squirrel, no tree squirrel, no grouse, and no ptarmigan, nothing. Ptarmigan all freeze this winter. All die. That's funny. Porcupine, all die, all together.

"That's the kind of story I have," he laughed softly and looked up from the recorder.

"Well, I like to see you, your sister, your mother. Your mother, that's my sister, Caroline. Same with your father, my real friend. Any man, remember God, that's my real friend, all the world round. Don't forget that, grandson. You remember. I remember. Thank you." And he was done.

Johnny spoke in Gwich'in to Sarah, who leaned close to the recorder. "Hello, *shitseii* (grandson) Teddy!" and spoke to him briefly in her language, which Johnny translated. Her message was much the same as his.

JOHNNY TURNED IN the trail. "See that hole?"

We were going grayling fishing. As always we carried rifles. Johnny had his model 95

Winchester, .30-.40 Krag, in a canvas and tanned moose-hide case slung over his shoulder. Rarely did a moose hunt occur like the one he described to Teddy on tape. Thus he repeated the story. They shared the food, much of it preserved as dry meat. A lot went to Venetie. Big animals and small, like the rabbits, were frequently absent for long periods. One obtained food whenever possible.

"That's a snake hole, sure," Johnny said. The hole was about a foot in diameter.

Johnny had told us before about the presence of huge snakes. Monster snakes.

"You ever see one?" I asked.

"No. I almost saw that snake once, big one! Maybe half-hour before I come. I saw track. If I see it, I'm going shoot it, all I can. Some little spit, maybe one drop will kill you. She only eat once every forty years. Eat anything."

I listened without response. We walked on. Stopping again he withdrew his deeply curved pipe from his coat. "Peterson pipe, best one," he grinned. It was well made with a worn silver band around the mid-section. He filled it with a mixture of Granger and chips of Black Bull twist tobacco. He wore an old army dress hat.

"Some places snake like lake, too. Eye that big, like plate. Maybe got hair on his head too."

We walked on, coming to the big creek behind the cabin. The ground was good and there was little water in the trail. Johnny wore high canvas boots with moose-skin soles. Over these as usual he wore rubber overshoes. Quietly we approached the creek bank, peeking over the edge into crystal clear pools. When we found large grayling, we cut long slender willows and attached lines. I started to shape a piece of willow leaf for bait. Johnny shook his head and handed me a little piece of fat. After we caught one, we'd use a small v-shaped sliver cut from beneath the grayling's throat for bait. Up the creek we walked quietly from pool to pool, drifting our baited hooks in front of our prey.

"*Gwinzii* (good)," he announced when we had caught eighteen or twenty grayling. We'd fished perhaps two hours. We returned to camp through clusters of small black spruce separated by stretches of dry tundra. We stopped on a small hill to nap in the warmth of the afternoon sun. A slight rustle woke me. An ermine stood on hind legs between Johnny and me, a foot away. In a second it disappeared, only to pop up again briefly to survey its invaders. This one still had its pure-white winter coat. It studied us alertly.

"*Avii*—weasel," Johnny chuckled.

We passed over a gravel bar where fresh caribou tracks led to a narrow pathway cutting through an otherwise steep bank. "Good place for snare, not far from cabin, too," Johnny said, putting down his pack and rifle. He fashioned a large loop with a thick strip of moose skin and secured one end to a tree. He worked for half an hour adjusting and camouflaging the opening until he was satisfied.

Back at Gold Camp, the three children ran to take our bags and empty the fish onto the cleaning table outside the cabin. They competed with one another, removing and eating the fish eyes, laughing gleefully.

"Today, below the creek, Johnny, we saw those old cabin ruins. Who lived there?"

"Well, nobody knows who. Long time ago maybe everybody die from some kind of sickness."

"Small pox?"

"Maybe. Used to be no sickness, before white man came. After Russians come, lots people die."

"You ever get sick?"

"Me? Yeah, I got flu, maybe in 1925. I was at Fort Yukon. My family was camped up Porcupine River twenty miles. Well, everybody start to get sick. Some old timers die. I start to be sick, too."

"I don't know for how many days, I feel hot. Then just feel cold. I can't sleep, can't eat. Well, I feel scared, for nothing."

"One man got boat with motor. I tell him, 'You take me across river, please. I need to go up river to my family.'"

"Did you walk upriver or go in boat?" The clock chimed in the background.

"That man just take me across the river. Then I walk up. I keep on going. I'm too cold. Well, I make fire but can't get warm. I want to sleep but I know if I sleep, I never get up. Just die right there. I keep on going. Two times I feel something go by, like spirit, see? That's my partners' spirit that go out when they die. They want me to go with them.

"I go on. Finally I see little sunshine on hill. My family is there. They almost got no food. I bring no grub. Well, my old lady and kids not sick but need food.

"I tell my wife, 'I try to go up to place where lots of ground squirrels.' I got big canoe. We go up by little lake where we see few ducks. She set a tent. I need to eat bird, something. I go in tent. Shotgun and .22 rifle right there. If I see anything I'm going to shoot.

"Well, by golly, one duck, one little duck. I don't know what white man call that duck—funny one. One place there is little grass. She go in there. I know she got nest, see? I take shotgun. I can't see duck but I shoot right in middle, kill duck. She got eggs with little ones inside.

"My old lady take off feathers. 'Big feathers, that's all,' I tell her, 'that small feather, leave it right there. Burn off little feathers all over. You boil it that way. Don't change it.'

"Well, I drink that hot duck juice, see? Just like life going into my body.

"I hear little ground squirrel make noise. I take number one steel traps and go out. On one side I use rifle and other side stick." Johnny gestures as though he is using a cane. "First time I make it to little log. Too weak, pretty near fall down.

"Hard work, forty yards, I make it. At every hole I set trap. I come back halfway, twenty yards. I got two sticks and finally (laughs) make it back to the tent.

"All the kids sick now, too. Nathaniel knock down like that." Johnny indicated him falling over with his hand. "Never moves, see. Try to put hot water in his mouth. I go check my traps. By golly, nine ground squirrel in traps, young ones! Well, I set traps again.

"Old lady, she burn off hair; she boil 'em. Take out guts but never skin, see? That's good medicine. I take juice. I get warm, all over. Same with all the kids. I try to not sleep. Try to get kids little something to drink. Pretty hard to wake them up, all right. I shake them all over. Drink half cup, every one of them.

"Second time, I go to traps. Nine again, young ones! Fort Yukon people find that out, too. Shoot tree squirrel. That's medicine, too.

"Down in Fort Yukon I don't know how many die. I think about eighteen or seventeen die in one day. All people, all over get sick. My two friends die, too.

"Long time ago, smallpox kill lots of people. At that time, pretty near all Chandalar Indians cleaned out. Three villages, pretty near nothing. All houses quiet, just like everybody sleep. The same time lots dogs die, too. Nobody to feed them. My grandpa's time."

Contagious diseases from Europe periodically swept through Gwich'in country. Transmitted northward along intertribal trade routes, they reached isolated areas long before white men arrived. In the latter half of the 1800s traders, explorers, missionaries, and gold-prospectors came in increasing numbers. Epidemics of smallpox, measles, diphtheria, and scarlet fever devastated Native families who had no immunity to these deadly infections.

Our week's visit passed quickly. The days were filled with chores: wood gathering, hauling water, setting snares, and fishing. We visited a lot, too, and there was always time for a story. We left with our charter to return to our normal regimented life. Elizabeth seemed to enjoy the visit.

OUR SON, DAVID, was born in the third week of August. I completed my commitment to the Public Health Service at Kanakanak in early September. From there we went to Nome where I worked for a month at the Methodist hospital. Before leaving Alaska to begin my orthopedic residency, we decided to visit Gold Camp to introduce David to Johnny and Sarah. It was late October. Our son was eight weeks old.

We chartered a Beaver aircraft on skis. Snow covered the gravel bar across from the cabins. The pilot flew low over the strip to get a good look. Johnny, Sarah, Maggie, and several children stood waving. An American flag hung from a nearby pole. The day was crisp and cold, about twenty-five below zero. Purple-tinged smoke rose from the cabin straight into blue sky. The plane circled the valley and lined up with the little strip. Snow filled the air from the prop wash as we touched down. We skidded to a stop just before the willows at the end of the strip.

Warm smiles greeted us as we climbed out of the plane. *"Neenjit doonch'yaa* (How are you)?"

"Hello, grandson, you wife, too. *Gwinzii, gwinzii."* Handshakes and hugs followed. In the cabin Maggie made a small hammock and hung it across one corner for David. Our baby was snuggled warmly in a rabbit fur sleeper that later became a parka. The bottom and sleeves were sown shut for now. One of the children gently swung the hammock.

Eyes were on Grandma Sarah as she went through the boxes of groceries we brought. "Camp robbers, just like camp robbers," she chuckled, passing oranges and candy to the excited kids. This was the nickname for the noisy gray jay that frequented camps, ready to steal food. They were welcome visitors in this lonely land.

"You see moose, caribou?" Johnny asked.

"No, nothing. We flew low over the mountain. I could see well. There were no tracks in the snow."

Liz and I shared the cabin with Johnny and Sarah. David slept in his hammock. There were few visitors, especially in winter. Maggie and her children had been there all fall. David was the center of attention.

"Grandpa and Grandma, will you be his godparents?" I asked Johnny and Sarah.

"Aaha, aaha," they nodded.

We visited there for four or five days. I was exhilarated. This was my first exposure to the Arctic winter and I was with a master. The Gwich'in had lived in this area of the world for some nine thousand to twelve thousand years, perhaps longer. They were the most northern Indian people in this hemisphere.

Johnny and I left the small cabin each day to hunt and gather wood. We entered a winter wonderland, acutely aware of the potential danger of the deadly cold. Days were short with the low-angle lighting tinting the mountaintops with a beautiful pink glow. The sky was deep blue, the air fresh and clean. There were no motors to disturb the silence. White dominated the world. There was no breeze. Dry snow stood on every twig and leaf in glistening, sparkling hills of crystals. Close observation revealed individual snowflakes. At these temperatures, twenty-five to forty-five degrees below zero, the snow was so dry it could not be compacted into a snowball. It creaked loudly beneath our knee-high Indian boots. Sarah had made a pair for me. The upper part was canvas with a foot of home-tanned moose skin. Inside were felt insoles and several layers of thick wool socks. They were warm and light.

We came upon an open stretch of water. It was thirty below. A dipper, a small sooty gray bird, flew to the edge of the water and disappeared into it.

"Johnny, how can that water not be frozen? How can that bird go into it?" Although I knew dippers fed underwater, I was amazed to see one at these temperatures.

"That stay open pretty near all year," Johnny said, without explanation.

We didn't kill anything. We hunted in the forest and in the open areas along the frozen creek that entered the river a half-mile below the cabins. I was enthralled by the beauty of the ever-changing, low-angle sunlight as it illuminated the snow and sparkled off crystals suspended in air. There were a few tracks of small animals. We stopped at each little trail, imagining the activity of the marten, rabbit, or squirrel that had passed this way, leaving delicate patterns in the snow. Silence prevailed. The squeak of our snowshoes in the dry snow was the only sound. Compared to the heavy commercially made snowshoes and boots I had worn, the Gwich'in-style snowshoes and winter boots that Johnny and Sarah made were light and gave me a sense of freedom rather than feeling like a burden.

Wood gathering was critical in the winter. There was only enough wood in the woodpile to last a few days. Each day we hooked two dogs to a homemade toboggan and went a mile or so on a well-packed trail to a stand of dead trees. There we cut and loaded the toboggan with small trees and let the dogs go. Even with the heavy load, they raced to the cabin, arriving long before we did. We worked and walked slowly so as not to sweat, as this could freeze in our clothes.

I was delighted to be there and cherished this experience. It was different for Liz, who found herself confined to a small crowded space with a two-month-old infant. She was a good sport but this was entirely alien to her. Only once did I persuade her to leave the cabin and go with us to get wood. On the way back she sat astride the small logs on the toboggan pulled by the two dogs. I was glad to see her smiling. I yearned for her to enjoy this experience.

Not until we were grounded by weather in Fort Yukon on the way home a few days later did I begin to realize how differently we felt. At fifty below, the planes were not flying, so we stayed in a small room on the second floor in Cliff Fairchild's Inn. A strained tension surrounded us. Elizabeth had grown up in urban Ohio and on Long Island. Even in the Peace Corps in Chile she lived in an urban area. I was raised in the rural South. She was anxious to return to civilization. I returned reluctantly.

I felt exhilarated in this vast, wild country so remote from modern society. Liz was not. She never returned to Gwich'in country. I was to return many times, drawn to the country and to this elderly couple who became my adopted grandparents and mentors.

WHEN THE TEMPERATURE rose after our unexpected delay in Fort Yukon, we flew to Fairbanks and then on to Seattle to pick up a new Volkswagen for the drive back to South Carolina.

The bus ride from the airport to downtown Seattle was an emotional experience for me. The paved roads, overpasses, traffic, and industrialization were overwhelming. I leaned my head against the window and gazed at the destruction we had brought to this land. Tears rolled silently down my cheeks. Clearly I visualized the contrast of sparkling snow, crisp cold pure air and the beauty of silence in Gold Camp with this stench and destruction of the natural world.

On the road several days later I was shocked to find a wide interstate highway cut through the redwood forest in northern California. From childhood I held a memory of being on a small, narrow road passing between towering giant redwoods with the sky hardly visible overhead. It was inconceivable that ancient trees had died to make way for a swath of grass and pavement. Later, in Berkeley, we visited former Peace Corps friends. On their table lay a book about the redwoods. I picked it up and found a before-and-after aerial photo of that section of the highway. The book advocated protection of the redwoods. I turned to the back cover to see who published it.

"What is the Sierra Club?" I asked my friend, Mike Kavanaugh.

Mike told me the Sierra Club was an environmental organization founded in the late 1800s by John Muir to protect special areas like Yosemite and Yellowstone. He added, "Now it takes on many issues. Protecting old-growth forests is one."

"How does one join?" I asked, immediately interested.

"There should be a form in the back."

I became a lifelong member. At that time I had never met an environmentalist. This was a crucial turning point for me.

CHAPTER 13

Orthopedic Residency

From San Francisco Bay we drove to Yosemite National Park to spend Thanksgiving week. There were few campers this time of year so the park service kept only one campground open. We found a site on the edge of the campground and pitched our tent. David seemed content snuggled in his rabbit fur sleeper. A yellow school bus arrived and teenagers piled out noisily and began shouting to one another and running about. Radios blared everywhere.

I walked out into a nearby meadow. The last rays of the sun bathed the majestic rock walls on one side; the opposite side stood in cold shadow, tinged with snow. The grandeur of Yosemite Valley swept away my irritation.

The place my folks found for us in South Carolina was perfect. The house sat in a three-acre pine forest on the shores of a narrow, winding lake five miles long. There was a neglected swimming pool and several out buildings. Beer bottles and trash littered the ground. It was the lake house of a local doctor who, due to ill health, had not used it for several years. The place needed work. The drive to the hospital took twenty minutes. Furman University was about the same.

During my four years of orthopedic residency, three at Greenville General and one at the Shriners' Hospital for Crippled Children, Liz got her teaching degree at Furman. She began teaching the chaotic year the public schools were integrated.

This was a time of great change in the South. My views were no longer in sync with the generally conservative medical staff. It was easy for the locals to dismiss the opinions of people from the north—they were Yankees, after all. I was angered by comments I heard after the assassinations of the Rev. Martin Luther King and Sen. Bobby Kennedy.

One busy night in the emergency room I was working with an excellent ER nurse. We were standing at the nursing station writing on charts when a door to the front office flew open and the receptionist exclaimed, "They shot Martin Luther King!"

The ER nurse responded, "Well, I hope they killed him!"

"Shut up and keep your opinions to yourself!" I responded harshly.

For the next few months the nurse spoke to me only as necessary and otherwise turned a cold shoulder. Then one day she asked me to check on the ER receptionist, who had just been in a car accident on the way to lunch.

"The ER doc saw her and is sending her for an x-ray of her clavicle, but she looks bad to me," the nurse said. "Would you please check her?"

The young woman was about to go by stretcher to radiology without a medical escort. She was deathly pale and her pulse rapid and weak. I found no bruise or deformity over her collarbone, though she felt the pain there. I raised the sheet. A large bruise overlay the left lower ribs. Her abdomen felt tense.

"IV fluids! She has a ruptured spleen and is going into shock." We started fluids with a large-bore needle and called general surgery. She went directly to surgery for an emergency splenectomy, a procedure to remove her damaged spleen.

The receptionist recovered quickly but would have died had the nurse not intervened. Without further discussion the nurse and I re-established a congenial professional relationship.

TWO EXCELLENT BLACK orthopedic cast technicians worked in the ER. They had years of practical experience and taught us much. All the residents respected them and were determined to get pay raises for them; in spite of their considerable skills, they were paid the same as orderlies who had much less responsibility and fewer skills. We pushed this issue for several years, finally getting as far as the hospital's board of directors. We failed to achieve our goal, as the two men predicted from the start.

One day I was working with both men. We were reducing a leg fracture and applying a plaster cast. The door opened and a nurse pleasantly requested, "When you finish here, would one of you boys go get a patient in x-ray?"

All three of us responded together, "No boys in here!" Mine was the only voice with rancor.

I loved orthopedics. There were many different surgical procedures. The diagnosis was usually apparent and the problem was how best to treat it. But it became clear to me that I could not remain in the South after four years of residency.

Our next stop was Montero in the lowlands of eastern Bolivia where I taught for five months in a small hospital, then on to Argentina for several months in a mini-fellowship in hand surgery with Dr. Eduardo Zancolli in Buenos Aires. Afterward, back in the states, I did a fellowship in arthritic surgery for five months in Denver with Dr. Mack Clayton, learning about artificial total joint replacements.

Meanwhile, I had been in frequent contact with Dr. Walter Johnson, medical director of the Alaska Native Medical Center, and Dr. Bob Grossheim, chief of orthopedics. Both encouraged me to endure the bureaucracy of Public Health Service headquarters in Maryland to apply for a staff position in Anchorage. I had expressed interest in the position annually for five years; it was not until the last week of the Denver fellowship that a job offer was confirmed. In July 1973 I joined the orthopedic department at ANMC, expecting to be the third orthopedist.

Bob Grossheim had been waiting for my arrival. "Thank God, now I can leave! I am burned out. I'm going into private practice with Doctor Mills."

"Dr. William Mills?" I asked. "The frostbite doc who developed the rapid re-warming treatment?"

"Yes, also known as the Admiral, his rank in the Naval Reserve. He and Von Wichman are the senior orthopedists in town. Doctor Mills is on the consultant staff here."

Doctor Grossheim took me on a tour of the hospital, explaining how the system worked. There was a serious backlog of orthopedic cases.

"At first I tried to clear the surgical backlog and hold clinics at the bush hospitals, but it was too much," he said, pulling out a drawer full of small scraps of paper with names on them. "Now I just try to care for the patients that come through the door. Here are names of people awaiting elective surgery. In case you can get to them."

"Locked knee," I read aloud, picking one case at random. The note was dated more than a year before. I felt dismayed. "And the other orthopedist?"

"Oh, he's staying. He is recovering from a thyroid psychosis. It's been a rough time. Fortunately there are two orthopedic residents here as part of their training program, which is based in San Francisco. They're a great help."

I was too busy to be depressed about the situation. Liz and I stayed in an apartment while we looked for a place to build a cabin. Anchorage was growing rapidly and land within commuting distance was becoming suburbia. We finally found an inholding in the huge Chugach State Park that surrounds Anchorage on three sides. The remote site had no electricity, running water, or phone service. There wasn't even a road at first. I'd have to use a mobile radiophone when I was on call at the hospital.

Having found a site for our future home I needed to find a builder. I called Jim Hitchcock, owner of Caribou Cabins in nearby Wasilla, whom a friend had recommended.

I'm looking for someone to build a small cabin near Anchorage," I told him.

"Come up and we'll talk about it," Jim responded.

Liz and I drove to Wasilla to meet Jim and share our vision of a log cabin with six hundred square feet of floor plus a sleeping loft. At first Jim was noncommittal but after an hour of discussion, he said, "I'll build your cabin. Let's take a look at your site. I can meet you there in a few days but it'll be January before I could start."

WORK WAS CONSUMING. In addition to the clinical work, I became department chief, "responsible for the orthopedic care of Alaska Natives," as my job description put it, but without any control over the budget or staffing.

Basic orthopedic instruments were available but it was difficult to obtain new systems. The administration did not understand that this was the beginning of a time of great change in my specialty. We did not have total joint implant systems, so hip and knee fusions were still the only option to offer for severe arthritis. Fusions relieve pain by making the joint stiff in one position. After the operation a patient spent months in a cast; for hip fusions, this required a body cast. I used much energy and time to get a total hip system. I chose the administrator of one of the rural hospitals for the first total hip replacement, and he became a strong advocate.

I soon learned from the residents that Doctor Mills disagreed with my treatment of certain pediatric orthopedic diseases. In a face-to-face encounter he implied that I was verging on malpractice treating a certain hip problem with crutch ambulation. I hotly retorted that he was the delinquent as he still put a child in a full-body cast with bed rest for two years.

It was frustrating to be criticized by Doctor Mills. Meanwhile, I had learned that I could not belong to the local orthopedic society because I was not on the staff at the private hospital. Somehow I posed a threat working for a salary rather than in a fee-for-service arrangement.

One of my patients, an ANMC internal medicine doctor, lost his leg below the knee in a motorcycle accident. I asked Doctor Mills for a consultation, as he personally had lived with a similar amputation for many years. After seeing the patient, Doctor Mills called to berate me. Angrily I hung up and drove across town to his office. His receptionist took one look at my face and ushered me into his office without delay. Framed diplomas, professional memberships, and awards certificates covered the richly paneled walls. It was a sharp contrast to our office with four desks crowded into one room and government green paint flaking from the walls.

As soon as Doctor Mills appeared, I unloaded my frustration. I was asking for his help but if he wanted to run the orthopedic department at ANMC, then he needed to be there, not become a distant critic. I was doing the best I could.

Surprised by my outburst, he laughed and this broke the tension. Our relationship improved. We became friends as well as mutually respectful colleagues.

CHAPTER 14

Lots of Stories

I felt anxious when Jim Hitchcock inspected our remote home site, which was perched on a steep slope. Would he be able to build there?

"It's possible," he said. "The road will be steep but I have an old army 'six-by.' We can haul in materials with it."

Liz visited all the Anchorage banks and savings and loans but could not get financing. I could not believe it. After all, I was a surgeon and a commissioned officer. My annual salary of $22,500 placed us in limbo—too much to qualify for mortgage assistance, yet not enough for a special loan to build a non-conventional home. We were able to start with a loan from my parents.

Jim's Caribou Cabins crew began to move in materials in late January 1974. The foundation had been completed. The logs, cut months before in the Tok area, were dried and peeled. At Jim's sawmill in Wasilla they were notched and three sides cut flat.

Jim was about five-foot-five, stout, strong, and competent. He had grown up on a homestead north of Anchorage and had been exposed to one narrow view of Native life. He had seen the highly visible urban street people, often drunk and filthy, and occasionally obnoxious. I, too, knew this side, as these individuals were frequent visitors to the emergency room. Often they spewed their anger and hatred at the medical staff. I was glad to know a different view and invited Jim to go to Gold Camp with David and me.

"I'd love to go," Jim said.

David, then six, Jim, and I flew on a Boeing 747 to Fairbanks where we boarded a Cessna Navaho for the flight to Fort Yukon. From there, we chartered a Cessna 175 on skis. We scheduled a pickup at Gold Camp in five days, weather permitting. It had been twenty-five to forty below the past week, and Tony, the pilot, told us not to expect a pickup if temperatures fell below minus fifty.

We flew low over the Yukon Flats, gained altitude near Big Lake, and crossed low over the hills to enter the East Fork valley. I rapidly scanned the valley and spotted a small column of rose-tinted smoke rising straight into the air from a tiny cabin. "There it is, upriver!" I pointed as the pilot banked toward it. As usual, a bright American flag hung limply on a tall spruce pole. Johnny and Sarah emerged from the main cabin. Three more people came out of the guest cabin. As we passed over they waved and I could see Stanley Frank. After circling the valley, we landed on the frozen slough near the cabins and climbed out.

"Hello, Johnny, I brought you some visitors!" Tony said.

"Good to see you," Johnny said, shaking hands.

I introduced Jim Hitchcock to Johnny and Stanley as Sarah took David's hand, "Grandchild, hello, grandchild! I'm glad to see you."

A young couple joined us.

"Hello, Mike, this is my wife, Mary Rose, from Arctic Village." The young man realized that I did not recognize him and laughed. "I'm Lawrence." Sarah and Johnny's grandson had been just seven when I first met him.

"Well, I certainly did not recognize you! It must be twelve years since I last saw you."

"Come, drink tea," Sarah motioned us toward the cabin. We crowded in and listened as Tony related the local news in Gwich'in country.

Then Tony stood and announced he must leave as he had a few more flights. The roar of the plane's engine reverberated against the hills. We watched until he was out of sight and stillness returned. We moved into Johnny and Sarah's cabin. I was glad the guest cabin was occupied as this would give us more time with them and more spontaneous stories from Johnny. Sure enough, after eating, Johnny brought out his pipe and asked Jim, "You like story?"

"Sure."

"Well, lots of stories." He was silent a while, smoking, then started.

"Used to be there was no land. Just one high mountain, like McKinley, up by North Slope. On top is level. All people were there. No land, see. Everywhere just water, all over. Lots people come up in canoe. They ask crow to find land.

"Well, you remember, crow is smart. Crow never have to kill anything. He always find everything ready, see? Wolf kill caribou or moose, crow eat it. Some rabbit that hawk or owl catch, crow eat that, too. Anything!" Johnny laughed. He always got a kick out of these stories. "That's why crow never have to kill animal ... too smart." He chuckled.

"Crow look for ground. Fly long way and just see water. Then in one place, he see something ... float up, sink down ... float up. That's ground, see?" Johnny slowly raised one hand palm up and then lowered it, palm down.

"Well, he try to catch little piece of ground but can't do it. Everybody try. One man got long spear ... you know, Eskimo use that kind to hunt for water animals. He say, 'You see that ground? It snake up, sink down all the time. You hit with spear, pretty hard.'

"Well, crow listen. Smart, see? Can use left hand just like right hand. They give him big meal. 'Sure, I try it,' crow say.

"He get in canoe. Put long spear on top the canoe, left side, not very far." Johnny mimics putting the spear down and paddling on one side, then the other, switching sides with every stroke. "Paddle like that. He got song, too." Johnny sang and paddled, a big smile on his face. "Well, crow watch, watch. He take spear in left hand, like that."

Johnny holds his left arm cocked. "Ground come up. When it start to sink down, crow hit it with spear!" Johnny laughed. "Well, lots people watch. The ground come up! Canoe is right on top ground. All people run down on ground. They leave everything on top the mountain—grub, everything. They run long way ... everybody happy.

"Crow walk up to their place. They leave lots of grease, all kind of food. Crow eat lots!" We both laugh. "That people forgot about crow, see? That's the way crow make land.

"There's other story, too. How it start. I tell you sometime. Well, sleep now."

Johnny filled the woodstove and went outside to fetch some more wood. Then he lit a small coal-oil lamp on the table and turned off the Coleman lantern that hung from a roof beam. The loud hiss of the lantern died and the mantle glow faded.

Johnny and Sarah settled back on the small platform of poles that served as both a bench seat and bed and pulled blankets over them. David and I slept on the other bench-bed. Jim spread his pad and sleeping bag on the floor.

The wood supply was low. After breakfast Stanley suggested, "Maybe we get wood today?"

I glanced at Jim. He nodded, so I said, "Sure. You want to go, David?"

"Yes, I'd like to go."

"Dress warmly then. I'm glad you're going!"

Jim sharpened a bow saw. Johnny watched a few minutes, then went out and returned with three or four more saws for Jim to sharpen. Stanley preheated the snow machine engine with a length of stovepipe angled from a Coleman stove and eventually got it started. He hooked up the toboggan and broke trail for a mile or so. We walked easily behind on the snow packed by the snow machine.

We warmed quickly cutting trees with handsaws and took off our parkas. The daytime temperature rose to twenty-five below. David's feet got cold. Stanley made a bed of spruce boughs for David to lie on and propped his feet up near a fire. Jim and I continued to cut while Stanley took loads to the cabins. After four loads we had sweated heavily, so we paused by the fire to dry off before heading back.

Johnny met us with a big smile, and Sarah said, "*Gwinzii*, good! Lots wood. Thank you. Come eat."

The next few days we cut the logs into stove-length pieces but spent most of the time in the cabin eating, dozing, and listening to Johnny or the radio. Lawrence had gone hunting. One night when we were almost ready for bed, Mary Rose came over and talked quietly with Johnny and Sarah in Gwich'in. Her voice was low and urgent, and they listened attentively.

When she finished, I asked what was the matter.

"Lawrence never come back," Johnny said. "Maybe he try to follow caribou and go too far. I go try to find him."

"I'll go, too," I said with some foreboding, as it was dark and the falling temperature was nearing fifty below. I got up and started to dress, as did Jim. We got ready in silence, putting on enough layers to keep out the cold. Sarah prepared food for Lawrence as well as a thermos of tea.

We donned parkas and went out. Johnny and I picked up rifles, which we kept outside so the actions wouldn't freeze from condensed moisture. We did not oil the rifles, since oil also freezes at these temperatures. It was overcast but we could see well enough by the diffuse light reflected from the snow. It was nearly midnight as we set forth. We solemnly followed Johnny onto the frozen river where the snow was not deep, then headed upriver on a snow machine trail in the eerie light.

We had not gone far when a ghostly apparition appeared out of the gloom. There was Lawrence, wearing a white canvas pullover over his parka. He walked steadily toward us carrying snowshoes under one arm and rifle in the other, giving no acknowledgment of our presence as he passed other than planting the snowshoes upright in the snow. He walked as if in a trance. We retrieved the snowshoes and followed him back to the cabin. No one said a word, but I'm sure the others shared the feeling that I did, not only glad for Lawrence's safe return but also relieved to avoid an ordeal ourselves.

In the cabin, after tea and soup, Lawrence began. "All week I've been hunting but I haven't even seen tracks. This morning I went way up. Suddenly several caribou crossed into the trees, too quick to get a shot. They were trotting, not too fast, so I follow them on trail snowshoes. Now and then they stop and I think I can catch up but I never do, and I go too far."

"Pretty hard. You can't do it," Johnny said, looking serious as he filled and lighted his pipe. "One time we got just little food. Not much. Those kids getting weak. I hunt every day, but nothing. No tracks. Not even tree squirrel. That time I'm strong, run fast on trail snowshoe, big one, that high." He indicated about four feet with his hand.

"Nobody beat me. Well, three caribou cross in front. Little deep snow. I follow. Long time I keep up. Start sweat but I can't stop. No food, see? We need it too much. Finally go too far. I know I can't make it back. Pretty near give out when caribou stop to eat. I shoot all three. Dark now, cold, too, I sweat too much. I need make fire but matches get little wet in my shirt pocket. That time we got different kind match, just one piece and you got to break' 'em off. Well, can't take chance. Can't stop, too much I sweat. Maybe freeze, see? I hold match in hand and go round and round tree. I get everything ready. Just got one chance. When match dry I try it, use whole match. I can't break off piece, my hands too cold.

"By golly, make big fire! Get warm, cook meat, use skin for blanket. Fresh skin freeze, just fold it. Cut spruce, make thick bed, skin blanket. Pretty near I'm done in. Danger, try to catch caribou.

"Well, Lawrence okay! Go to bed now. I smoke first."

ON THE WAY back to Anchorage, Jim turned to me, "I can't tell you how much this meant to me. I see Indians differently now."

"What struck you most?"

"Getting firewood. On the homestead we always cut cords of firewood to store for the winter. I thought Indians were too lazy to do this. Now I see their way gets you out and keeps you active all winter."

"Yeah, you don't put off going for firewood when the woodpile gets low. At those temperatures you don't want the fire to go out."

Jim continued. "And the tiny cabin, sufficient, easy to heat, and they have basic comforts. Most of it is hard to explain."

"Well you can see what an influence they've had on me. I'm glad you went."

CHAPTER 15

Thanksgiving

David, by then seven years old, and I decided to spend Thanksgiving 1974 with Johnny and Sarah. After sending a message on Trapline Chatter that we were coming, we flew to Fort Yukon and chartered a Cessna 172 on skis to Gold Camp. Our pilot, Tony, was still flying for Air North. It was forty-five below zero. The air was completely still.

"I won't be able to stop my engine for more than a few moments, if at all," Tony told us.

We flew over the flats and crossed the Porcupine River. Splotches of dark spruce contrasted with the white world below, the outlines of streams and lakes barely visible through the snow. Moose tracks traversed a few lakes. Occasionally our flight crossed over the trail to Venetie and we once spotted a snow machine towing a toboggan; two souls traveling through a vast wilderness area. We angled over the foothills and entered the East Fork valley. As we buzzed low over the cabins, we saw that the frozen slough had been packed and marked with spruce boughs as a landing strip. Tony circled, studying the strip. Johnny and Sarah stood outside. Around we came and down, hitting the snow smoothly.

As we quickly decelerated, Tony shouted above the engine noise, "It's soft. When we pull around, get out quickly with your gear. I'm not going to stop. I'll pick you up in five days, weather permitting, but pack this strip!"

We jumped out and sank into knee-deep snow. Johnny had tried to pack it on snowshoes, but the cold, dry snow resisted compression. When Johnny appeared, Tony quickly handed him a turkey. "Can't stop—too cold—snow is too deep! Happy Thanksgiving!"

David and I quickly pulled out our gear and closed the doors. Tony gunned the engine and Johnny and I rocked the plane around on the snow for takeoff. Snow from the prop wash suddenly blew back my parka hood and lashed my face with a small blizzard, bitterly cold. I reeled back, the skis broke free, and the plane raced down the frozen river gaining speed and rising slowly into the air, the roar of its engine reverberating against the hills.

Stepping back, my right foot suddenly broke through into water. It was only knee deep but a complete surprise. Water at fifty below? We headed for the nearby cabins.

Johnny shook his head, "You don't see my stick?" He pointed at a small dead spruce pole, standing inverted to show it had been purposefully placed as a marker. "Open water," he said.

By the time we walked a couple hundred yards to the cabin, ice had encased my outer pants and knee-high army mukluks. Inside the frozen casing I was warm.

Sarah greeted us warmly. "Grandchild, good to see you. You son, too." She took our hands gently. Johnny tossed the frozen turkey into the cache beside the cabin.

"I thought maybe you don't come. Too cold."

"We were lucky Tony was flying. He was willing to bring us."

The cabin was hot. The fifty-five-gallon drum stove took up an appreciable amount of space in the twelve-by-fourteen-foot cabin we helped build years before. An old door served as a table with pole platforms on either side for sitting or sleeping. A stump was carved into a stool.

As my clothes thawed, a puddle formed on the floor. "Dry the floor good," Johnny reminded me. One had to be careful to keep soft tanned moose-skin boot soles dry or they froze and lost their insulation. A broom was always left at the door for carefully brushing dry snow from one's boots upon entering.

Johnny opened the door. The cabin cooled quickly and we entered a cycle that was repeated again and again into the evening. With the door closed, the heat gradually increased so that clothes came off layer by layer until we were down to an undershirt. Then Johnny or Sarah would open the door and a dense white fog would sweep across the doorsill covering the floor. As it got colder, on went a shirt, then a sweater. Finally one of them would close the door, and the heating would begin again. David and I learned not to interfere.

I was careful to stay on the packed trails. Because of everyone's heavy meat diet, the outhouse was odiferous, even at forty below. A wicked-looking frozen pyramid rose like a stalagmite. When this reached seat level—the seat being composed of crossed poles—it had to be broken off. I decided to go off the trail a ways and step into the brush. The extremely dry snow at this temperature does not pack. I stepped off into about six feet of dry fluff and found myself floundering helplessly. It was difficult to pull myself upright and climb back onto the trail. Thereafter I used the outhouse. Johnny laughed when he saw where I had thrashed in the snow.

During the short winter day Johnny and I went for firewood with a toboggan and two dogs. The winter trail behind the cabin led across what had been a swampy area in summer and on a few miles to a stand of dead trees. On this visit I cut trees with a bow saw and Johnny de-limbed them with an ax. We put a load on the toboggan and the dogs pulled it back to the cabin ahead of us.

Wood gathering got us outside. There was no choice. Johnny cut wood as needed. He went quite a distance from the cabin, farther than he needed to go.

"I keep these trees nearby for when I get old, don't have to go far," he said. I wondered when that might be as he was nearly ninety.

Being outside was always enjoyable. Marten hat, parka, long johns and pants with Gwich'in boots kept us warm and were pleasantly light. Snow particles sparkled like tiny diamonds in the winter sunlight. We always carried our rifles with us in hope of coming across a moose. But they were few and far between. We saw no tracks other than our own.

Sarah was accustomed to spending her days in or near the cabin. During our visit, the thermometer on the outer cabin wall ranged from a high of minus forty-five to fifty-eight below. I encouraged David to join us but most days he balked. His mood got progressively worse. He'd read everything available including Johnny's copy of *The Chandalar Kutchin,* by Robert McKennan, published by the Arctic Institute of North America in 1965. McKennan, an anthropologist, had come to Gwich'in country in 1933. Johnny has been one of his main informants. Included in the book was a great photo of Johnny and quite a few of his stories.

One evening as Johnny told stories, I spoke to David, "Listen to this story. It's really good."

David sat forward on the bed but as Johnny started, he flopped back. "I've already heard that one."

This was too much for me. I revered my time with Johnny and Sarah. "Tomorrow you are going outside with me." I tried to keep the irritation out of my voice.

The next day after breakfast, I spoke to David, "Get dressed and let's go out."

"It's too cold," he whined.

"Get dressed. Put on two or three layers of long johns. You've got your marten hat, rabbit parka and moose-skin boots. You will be warm." My voice hardened but I kept the volume low.

"I don't want to."

"Get dressed. I didn't ask if you wanted to." I spoke in hard tones. Johnny and Sarah were silent. I was aware that this was not their way. David dressed and we went out into the brief dazzling day and walked along the frozen river. It took but a few minutes' exposure to this silent wonderland, so far from the stench and noise of engines and the press of civilization, for my son's mood to lighten completely. We laughed; life was good. A frozen patch appeared on his left cheek.

"We better go back. Your cheek is freezing."

"Not yet."

We returned happy and joking. His sour spell was gone. Johnny did not admonish me until that evening after supper. David had pushed back on the pole bed and was napping.

As Johnny prepared his pipe, he said, "Don't get mad you boy. No use."

"He needed to get out ..." I began.

"No use," he interrupted in a tone that sought no argument. "No use to get mad you boy."

ON THANKSGIVING MORNING I asked if I should get the turkey from the cache. I had seen no fresh meat. In Venetie it had become commonplace to have turkey on Thanksgiving. Clara and Jessie John, the first young people from the village to attend high school at Mt. Edgecombe in Sitka, had enjoyed the Thanksgiving dinner tradition there and brought it home with them.

"No," Johnny said. "We go get wood."

Later the four of us sat to a dinner of potatoes, bannock, cooked apples, and a mystery meat stew. It was good. I did not recognize the meat or the bones.

"What kind of meat is this? It's good!"

Sarah replied, "Lynx," which she pronounced "link."

"Hmmm," I mused. I'd not known lynx to be an animal that Gwich'in ate. Eating cat seemed unusual. We ate with relish, however. "Good Thanksgiving today. I'm glad to be here."

"*Aaha*. Me, too. I'm glad, grandson," Sarah said.

THE MIDWINTER DAYS were short. The sun was visible an hour and a half; twilight doubled daylight to three hours. But it was never really dark. Whiteness dominated the world. We walked along the river looking for a way to cross.

The snow was not yet deep; we wore Johnny's small homemade trail snowshoes, which were light and well made. The strapping that held our feet to the frame was tanned moose skin arranged in a simple, effective manner that allowed one to twist the Native winter boot securely into it without leaning over or using one's hand.

The night before, Johnny had announced, "Maybe moose is up on mountain. Tomorrow we go look." We had not seen any fresh tracks on this side of the river.

We came to a natural ice bridge, partially covered with snow, over the main channel of the East Fork. It was about twenty feet wide, arching forty or fifty feet over a torrent of water. Johnny leaned forward and tapped the ice soundly with his walking stick, nearby at first, then farther out.

"Good sound. I think it's okay. You wait. I go first, then I tell you." He seemed sure. I trusted his judgment.

He crossed, gently tapping before him with his stick, judging the ice by sound and vibration. Johnny did not swim, not that it would have helped if he fell in. Getting swept under the ice would kill anyone quickly. Once he was across, I followed.

We kept the pace slow and steady, careful not to sweat. At thirty below I had my parka open. We climbed for over an hour, gradually nearing the rounded top of the mountain. He pulled out his pipe and began the ritual of getting it going.

"Too old, I'm getting too old. Sure, I know moose in little meadow on other side near top." I understood the implication but did not respond. He smoked his pipe, waiting.

"Too old, me." He knocked ashes from the pipe. We waited. "Not far ... maybe little bit far."

These rounded hilltops went on forever. Our tracks were the only ones I saw. We stood there. I remained silent.

"Well, what you think?" he finally asked.

"I go back with you." I had no desire to continue wandering about looking for a meadow I had never seen, shoot a moose there, and then recross the river alone with a load of moose meat. Daylight was fading. I knew he was disappointed but he said nothing. We returned to camp with no meat.

I had arranged a charter flight to Fort Yukon the next day. As we flew low over the mountaintop in the single-engine Cessna, I used a credit card to scrape frost from a window. Through this peephole I scanned the land below. Three moose browsed in a meadow just down the other side of the mountain.

Johnny and Sarah at Gold Camp in 1974.
Photo by Mike Holloway.

Venetie in 1961.

Photo by Ted Holloway.

Mike and Johnny taking a smoke break.
Photo by Ted Holloway.

Volk and Johnny's dog Blackie.
Photo by Ted Holloway.

Stanley Frank setting a rabbit snare.
Photo by Ted Holloway.

Mike and Stanley making the firewood raft.
Photo by Richard Volkwein.

Rafting the firewood down to Gold Camp.
Photo by Richard Volkwein.

Volk and Mike cooking bear meat in camp.
Photo by Ted Holloway.

Mike and Johnny stretching out the bear hide.
Photo by Ted Holloway.

Ted, Johnny and Mike with the pack dogs at Ackerman Lake.
Photo by Richard Volkwein.

Stanley, Johnny, Mike and Volk work on the frame for what may be the last moose-skin boat used in Alaska.
Photo by Ted Holloway.

Johnny carving a pilot paddle for the moose-skin boat.
Photo by Ted Holloway.

The finished moose-skin boat.
Photo by Ted Holloway.

Richard Birchell, some children and Abraham Christian see us off as we leave Venetie.
Photo by Ted Holloway.

Back row from left to right; Hamel, Lawrence, Maggie, Sarah, Johnny and Jimmy Roberts in front of two cords of firewood we cut. *Photo by Ted Holloway.*

Johnny, Mike and the pack dogs leaving Venetie for Gold Camp.
Photo by Richard Birchell.

Willy and Mike listen as Johnny tells a story.
Photo by Ted Holloway.

Aerial view of Gold Camp in May of 1967.
Photo by Mike Holloway.

Gold Camp in the winter of 1967.
Photo by Mike Holloway.

Sarah holding baby David.
Photo by Mike Holloway.

Johnny walking down a winter trail.
Photo by Mike Holloway.

Johnny fishing for grayling.
Photo by Mike Holloway.

David's birthday.
Photo by Mike Holloway.

David getting warmed up while we cut firewood.
Photo by Mike Holloway.

Maggie Frank Roberts in 1982.
Photo by Ted Holloway.

Mike and Sarah in Venetie.
Photo by Margie Ann Gibson.

Jenny Sam gives Margie some new gloves in Venetie.
Photo by Mike Holloway.

From left to right; Dan, Maggie, Hamel and Nathaniel in 1988.
Photo by Mike Holloway.

CHAPTER 16

David's Birthday

In late August 1975 David and I flew to Arctic Village. After unloading our gear alongside the gravel airstrip, we made several trips moving everything down to the river. A large sign declared this to be Gwich'in Indian Country. All visitors must sign in at the Arctic Village Council office. We walked the mile or so into the village, which consisted of perhaps forty cabins scattered over the small hills along the upper East Fork of the Chandalar River. Autumn colors were beginning to show. Small calm lakes reflected the colors. A craggy mountain rose across the river. Several young men sped by on three-wheeled all-terrain vehicles leaving a trail of dust.

In the council office, a young man about twenty sat behind a desk, a scowl on his face. A red bandanna about his forehead bound his shoulder-length straight black hair. I thought of his relatives, the Apache, far to the south.

"What do you want? Are you here to hunt sheep?" His tone was not friendly. Often "sport" hunters passed through Arctic Village on their way to hunt in the Arctic National Wildlife Range to the north. Many of them were on leave from military bases near Fairbanks and Anchorage.

"No. We want to float the river down to Venetie. Do we need a permit?"

"Well, how many days are you going to camp on our land?" His manner was brusque. "The land on this side of the river is Gwich'in. It's five dollars a night to camp on our land."

"We will be on the river about ten nights. We'll stop at Gold Camp to spend time with Johnny and Sarah Frank. I'll pay for all ten."

His manner abruptly changed. "You don't need to do that! There are plenty of good camping places on the other side, and that's not reservation land."

The reservation had become Gwich'in land with Congressional passage of the Alaska Native Claims Settlement Act in 1971. Venetie and Arctic Village had rejected a monetary settlement and opted out of the complicated system of regional and village Native corporations set up by the act. Instead they chose to manage their land settlement with a traditional tribal government.

"I'll pay for ten nights. That way we'll have the choice."

He wrote a receipt.

We strolled up to the store, a frame building that contrasted with the log homes and the elegant log church across the road. I knew few people here. The Sam family had moved here from Venetie. I inquired about my "sister" Jenny Sam, and her husband Moses. They were away so we headed back down to the river to put up our camp.

The next morning was clear. "Let's go into town," I said. "I saw a coffee shop sign yesterday. We can meet a few people." I figured we had plenty of time to get to Gold Camp in time for David's eighth birthday.

"Sure," he answered.

"Where is it?" David asked, looking around after we got back to the village.

I pointed to a sign on a nearby cabin. We went in the open door. Three or four men sat around.

"Neenjit doonch'yaa?" I greeted.

"Gwinzii," they responded.

A large stainless coffeepot sat on the counter. I filled two cups, passing one to David. We sat quietly sipping coffee. After a time one of the men asked us in a friendly tone, "Where are you from? Where are you going?"

"Down the East Fork to visit Johnny and Sarah Frank, then on to Venetie. We have a kayak, like a canoe."

"Some places there are lots of rocks and fast water, not like here," somebody said. Introductions followed.

"You know Johnny and Sarah?" Steven Peter asked. An elderly gentleman, Steven wore a blue cap with a small white bow above the bill, a style favored by men of his generation.

"I have known them for a long time. They are David's godparents."

We chatted awhile. A few people drifted in and out, often wordlessly taking a cup of coffee.

One asked, "You see that light on the mountain last night?"

"Oh, yes, the lightning." We rarely saw lightening in the coastal area near Anchorage. I thought it was more common in the Interior.

"What cause that?"

My answer of an electrical charge building up and releasing seemed quite unsatisfactory. I stood and reached into my pocket, "How much for four cups?" I saw quizzical expressions so I pointed toward the coffee shop sign.

Laughter broke out. "That's old, that sign. No coffee house for a long time! This is my house," Steven replied.

"Well," I stammered, "I'm sorry. We wouldn't have come in... ."

"No. Don't worry."

David looked at me and shrugged. I imagined the reception an Indian would receive walking into a home in Anchorage or Fairbanks and helping himself to a cup of coffee.

"*Mahsi' choo* (big thank you)," I said, still embarrassed.

"Be careful. Watch out for rocks."

THERE WAS LITTLE current in the river at first so we paddled steadily. In this river basin the tree line extended much farther north than in most regions of the Arctic. The spruce trees were four or five inches in diameter near the village and some grew twenty feet tall. Johnny had told me the trees were getting bigger, that they had been only head high when he was young. Brush was getting thicker on mountaintops, too, where once only lichen and tundra grew. Moose were seen farther up the rivers and they were more plentiful.

The water was crystal clear. Mosquitoes had died out in mid-August and were replaced by "no-see-um" gnats, but they were not bothersome on the river. It was good to be alone with David. I was the only orthopedist with the Public Health Service at Alaska Native Medical Center in Anchorage and severely overworked. For more than a year we had been short two orthopedists in spite of intense recruiting efforts. It was hard to compete with the high incomes offered in private practice. When I took time off, two private orthopedists in Anchorage helped the two residents with emergencies.

By late afternoon the current increased. In the river bends were "rock gardens" with many boulders to maneuver around. An accident could become serious quickly in the cold water. The remote area saw few travelers.

The next four or five days were idyllic. We floated fifteen to twenty miles a day. It was about eighty miles on the sinuous river to Gold Camp. The weather remained clear and crisp. Fall was in the air and the colors changed daily, spurred on by a light frost at night.

David had learned gun safety and handled the .22 Winchester well. Occasionally we saw spruce grouse. "It's okay if you want to shoot a grouse; we'll eat it," I told him.

David looked thoughtful a few moments, and then said, "We don't need it though, so I won't." We still had some caribou meat that Jenny Sam's son Timothy gave us.

This was my first time on the river above Gold Camp. It had been thirteen years since I last hiked there from Venetie. As we got closer I watched carefully so we wouldn't float past it. The cabins would not be visible as we sat low in our kayak on the river. Rounding a bend we came upon a five-gallon Blazo can suspended on the end of a long pole. We pulled in. A note taped to the can announced "Gold Camp Johnny Frank Aug 18." It had been written five days before. Standing, I saw the familiar cabins and the American flag across the gravel bars.

Johnny and Sarah stood outside as we approached, broad smiles on their faces. *"Neenjit doonch'yaa?* Good to see you, *shitseii* (grandson)." Sarah took our hands in hers. "Drink tea." She pointed to the kettle on the oil-drum stove.

"How come you put up that can?" I inquired.

"I think maybe you miss it, go too far."

"But I never told you when, or even if, I'd come."

"Aaha," he replied, smiling.

When I visited in January, I had said maybe David and I would come down the river that summer. He advised we not come in June when the water was too high. I had intended to send a radio message on Trapline Chatter but had not gotten around to it.

"Did you ever do that before, put up a marker?"

"No. First time." Johnny and Sarah laughed.

After supper Sarah said, "No meat, no meat. Just fish and rabbit. Old man get too old to hunt. Can't see good, too."

Johnny took the pipe from his mouth and looked at me. "Today brown bear come up on gravel bar, just below, in willows. I try to shoot him but no good. Sun right here," he indicated it in his eyes. "Just wound it. I follow it down to the creek where he crossed. Tomorrow we look for bear."

This announcement and his casual attitude surprised me. "Will tomorrow be okay? We still have plenty of daylight today."

"Tomorrow okay. After breakfast."

"Tomorrow is David's birthday, too."

In the morning, I checked out the rifles in the cache as I had brought only the .22. I selected a well-used Model 70 Winchester, .30-06, and cleaned it. After a leisurely breakfast and several cups of tea, Johnny announced, "Maybe we go look for bear now."

As we got things together, David stood around and finally asked, "Can I go, too?"

Before I could say no Johnny said, "Sure."

Though apprehensive, I accepted his judgment. I had almost answered that this was dangerous and thus "man's work." We took *Daanduu* (devil), Stanley's funny-looking little mongrel dog, and one other dog through the woods to the creek and crossed in the canvas boat to where Johnny had tracked the bear. *Daanduu* began to sniff about and Johnny found a few drops of dried blood. Then the dogs headed into the woods and we followed. Now and then *Daanduu* stopped to sniff and at these spots we'd find some fresh sign—a turned over rock or log, scuffed moss, a drop of blood.

Several miles downriver both dogs suddenly began running and, for the first time, barking. We ran out to the top of a cut bank to get a clear view downriver. The grizzly was running across gravel bars from the forest toward the river, limping on one front leg but moving fast. At the edge of the river he stood on hind legs looking across. Here there was only a single channel and the current was very fast. The bear considered swimming before turning to run back toward the woods at a right angle to us. I dropped to a sitting position and we both began to shoot. Johnny had a .30-.30. I'd wondered why he hadn't brought his favorite rifle, the .30-.40 Krag. Just before the bear reentered the cover of the forest, it collapsed in a small stream, rolled to its back, and was still. I approached only when Johnny said okay.

We skinned the bear. I used an Old Hickory butcher knife that I carried in a sheath given to me by Stanley Frank. Its beadwork depicted card suits and Stanley's initials. The greatest benefit of my being here was to pack the meat. In nomadic days the family simply would have moved their camp to the carcass. Johnny put a few choice parts in his pack. David took my rifle. I cut a pole five feet long and put a front quarter on each end to carry over my shoulder. I wanted to make as few trips as possible.

Johnny watched and said, "No good."

"I'll try it."

Johnny shook his head and we set off. The first few steps were okay. The pole balanced over my shoulder with one quarter in front and one behind. Slowly they began to swing in opposite directions as I walked, soon creating a pendulum effect that increased until it threw me off balance. Then I'd stop, stabilize the load, and start again, repeating the cycle. Johnny didn't look back or make any comment. It was a long way to the cabins.

Sarah was pleased to see us. With a big smile she repeated, *"Gwenzii, gwenzii.* Now we got meat!"

It took me several days to pack all the meat back to Gold Camp. I'd take a hook and bring back grayling, too. My emotions were unsettled. My older brother, Bill, and I shared a single-shot .410 shotgun when I was seven. We had bird dogs and rabbit dogs. Hunting got us outdoors and brought companionship with our father. We learned to respect the animals we hunted and to not waste anything we killed. I cried when I killed my first squirrels but kept hunting.

Two African-American families sharecropped on our farm back then. Clyde Jesse, who was a year older than I, became a friend and hunting companion. His family always welcomed food from our hunts. His father, Tobe, would ask us to bring him robin breasts when large flocks flew through in the spring. We'd hunt them with a pellet rifle, taking turns shooting, even though in my family harming songbirds was forbidden.

When I worked in the hospital at Kanakanak on Bristol Bay, I could leave my apartment on cross-country skis and, once beyond a nearby hilltop, enter a pristine world of whiteness and rolling tundra out of sight of the village. In five or six miles I'd come to clumps of willows in small drainages. There I hunted ptarmigan—white birds against the snow and then a splatter of bright red blood on white. Occasionally when a ghostly snowy owl hunted the same area, I would stand in my skis watching and give it preference.

During my orthopedic residency in South Carolina we were not far from the family farm. I hunted when possible. One day I was bird hunting and killed four quail on a rise, unusually good shooting for me. As I picked them up, something in me changed. Why had I taken these lives? Even though we would eat them, I realized, we did not need them. At that instant I became a non-hunter.

Near the end of my four-year residency, Liz went to the used-car dealer in my hometown to sell back an old Ford sedan. She met resistance from the salesmen. "Mr. White told my husband, Mike Holloway, that you'd buy it back at the end of four years," she told him.

They went to the office to discuss it with Mr. White.

"Which Holloway boy is that?" he asked. "I get the three confused."

"He is the one that quit hunting," a salesman responded.

This story amazed me. I hardly knew the man.

Yet when we stalked the bear I was all hunter again, acutely alert, cautious, and ready to kill. When we saw the bear, my response was automatic—the run to get a clear shot, dropping to a stable sitting position, and shooting three or four times, smoothly working the bolt-action rifle. A feeling of deep fulfillment came with providing food needed for survival. For all my philosophy I was a hunter-killer but I would only hunt here and for these reasons.

While I packed meat, David stayed in camp. For his birthday, Johnny and Sarah gave him a large wolverine skin, which he prized. He seemed to enjoy doing chores or whittling on a piece of spruce. In photos I took of the three of them, David has the fur draped over his shoulder, a big smile on his face, his eyes almost obscured by his long hair. Sarah dried much of the bear meat. As she sat on the ground working, we cut grass and cleaned up around the cabins. When I picked up some old caribou hooves and tossed them into the fire, Sarah immediately reached in to retrieve them.

"No," she said. "Save for hard time. Starvation time. Use for soup."

"Old lady worry," Johnny said. "Maybe not enough meat. There is little moose lake down past where we take bear. Maybe moose come there."

"You want me to go down and see?"

"Little bit far. Old trail. Maybe you won't find it. Maybe seven, no, six miles."

"We can go, then, so I can pack meat." I didn't relish the thought of packing a moose that far.

We set out the next morning, a bright, clear day, packing rifles and a little food.

"Take dog?" I asked.

"No. Maybe scare moose," Johnny replied.

The tundra was dry. The mosquitoes were gone and no-see-ums were graciously absent. We walked slowly but steadily, stopping now and then to rest. In mid-afternoon we arrived at the lake. Moose tracks were plentiful and fresh. But no moose. The lake was perhaps two or three acres and surrounded by a border of green sedges. A small stream flowed from it toward the river, now a mile or two away. *Ddhah Dzak* loomed downriver. It still gave me a shudder, perhaps from its dark connotations. It seemed sinister. Most mountains invite exploration or climbing—this one did not.

"I tell you time Ginnis, Ginnis Golen, shoot bush man?" Johnny asked. "We call it *Naa'in* ... up on side of *Ddhah Dzak*. Ginnis camped up on the side, fall time, hunting caribou. He got tent, pot, food—everything. Sometime when he come back to camp, something little funny, something missing or moved. He killed caribou; ribs disappeared, later sugar gone. He knows somebody watch him. He wait, rifle ready, but nothing. Just Ginnis there; two other men already go back to Venetie.

"One day Ginnis sitting on rock, waiting for moose. He sees *Naa'in,* look like man. Ginnis scared. He shoots and hit him. *Naa'in* jump up in air and fall down. Look dead, see? Ginnis don't even go back to camp. He leave everything there. Go down Venetie fast, never rest, never stop. On down to fish camp. *Naa'in* maybe magic, see? Nobody shoot *Naa'in*."

"Did anything happen to Ginnis?"

"Well, not then, but he worry all time."

Johnny was in Venetie years later when someone found Ginnis in his cabin, dead from a gunshot wound. People talked about suicide.

"I go there first thing. Chain on door—on outside, see? He can't do it. Maybe he pay somebody to do it. Funny, house next door. Nobody say anything."

"SURE, I KNOW big bull moose come here in the morning." Johnny said. "Too bad we got no grub, not even tea."

"I can stay here," I volunteered. "I got a hook. I can catch grayling."

"No. Better we go back." We started a small fire and made Canadian tea.

"I'll be okay—no problem," I said. Johnny didn't argue. The stream was but a yard wide. I moved along it cautiously and in the next hour caught a half-dozen grayling. By then I thought Johnny had left so I was surprised to find that he had only moved farther into the woods, where he sat by a fire waiting for me.

"I wait on you."

"Well, I can stay."

He didn't answer or move. I realized that he would not leave me here alone, so I drank a little tea and we left. On the return to Gold Camp we lost the trail through the tussocks. The going was dry but tiring. We went slowly and stopped often. Johnny was running out of energy.

"I take your rifle," I offered. He had the heavy model '95 Winchester.

"No."

With each rest, I became more concerned. I'd never seen him like this. When we started again I picked up his rifle. He did not object. Finally we got to the creek, where I brought the canvas boat to him and helped him in. He was barely able to stand. The water was just high enough in the slough to float him and the boat. I waded alongside and pulled the boat as close to the cabin as we could get. Sarah looked worried as I helped him up the bank.

"Too old, too old," she said with concern.

Johnny collapsed on his bed, immediately asleep.

"You eat," Sarah said, placing a bowl of boiled bear and macaroni before me. I ate, drank tea, and then fell asleep, too. When I woke four hours later, Johnny sat at the table drinking tea. He looked fully recovered.

"Pretty near I'm all done in!" he laughed. "Now I'm okay. I drink lots of tea ... lots of sugar, too!"

DAVID AND I got a late start leaving Gold Camp on a clear, brisk fall day. The sun was obscured and it was cold as we made our way downriver in the kayak. That night we camped on the riverbank where a small stream flowed from the flank of *Ddhah Dzak,* which was wrapped in mist and clouds. The temperature was falling rapidly. It was a poor campsite with little firewood, crowded between thick brush and the river. In the early morning light we saw that ice had formed along the edge of the river.

We stopped frequently to make fires. On the way downriver from Arctic Village, David had paddled, sang, and was active. Now he was immobile, which frightened me, and I worried that he was becoming hypothermic. I gave David some hard candy and urged him to sing and paddle. After he thawed at a fire, I encouraged him to practice shooting the .22— anything to stay active. We had no trouble on the river, though there were many sweepers. Now I understood the reality of the term "termination dust." This was the first dusting of snow on the mountains, historically a sign for early miners to leave the backcountry, fast.

In Anchorage this time of year we joked that it was time for "snowbirds" to head south for the winter.

It was a relief when we dragged the kayak up on the bank in Venetie near Jessie (John) and Albert Williams' cabin and accepted an invitation for tea.

CHAPTER 17

Winter Camp

I was in Gold Camp the following February when Stanley Frank arrived by snow machine. Traveling alone, he had to break trail nearly the whole way from Venetie. Several days later we headed upriver. Johnny wanted us to set up a tent for a hunting camp. Stanley drove while I hung onto the back of the toboggan that trailed behind, standing on the short runners and holding on to sawed-off handles. The snow sparkled in the sun, millions of tiny reflectors. Crystals lay on the branches and hung suspended in the air. In this fairyland, the sound and smell of the machine were offensive. Such a contrast to hunting with Johnny!

Few had working dog teams. Those remaining were mostly for racing—or simply kept by habit, but little used. By the 1970s, the snow machine had become the primary method of winter travel in bush Alaska. Frozen rivers became winter highways, and the Native people traveled sometimes hundreds of miles between villages, hunting en route. It didn't take long to go ten or twelve miles with a toboggan full of winter gear. These machines were practical for hunting, hauling wood, or visiting.

Upriver, the white canvas wall tent went up quickly. This was a regular camping spot and the poles were there already. We set up the little wood stove and ran the metal chimney pipe up through the roof. A metal piece sewn into the roof protected the tent from catching fire. After starting up the stove, we cut armfuls of spruce boughs and covered the floor with a thick layer. Then Stanley cut slices from a caribou front quarter he'd brought. As the meat sizzled in the frying pan, snow melted in the kettle for tea.

"Pretty good! Okay, huh?" Stanley smiled.

"Sure is. This is the way to winter camp," I agreed.

It was an understatement. The tent was warm; the aroma of the caribou frying mingled with the scent of the spruce boughs. It was a sanctuary. I lay back on the green cushion, protected from the cold earth. I imagined how difficult it had been in the "old days" when families and clans moved frequently, pulling all the gear and looking for food while packing the children and the elderly.

It was a pleasure to see Stanley again. We had become good friends. He didn't talk much but possessed a great sense of humor, a soft voice, and gentle manner. He was popular with women but had never married. He visited Gold Camp periodically to check on his grandparents and hunt, cut firewood, and do whatever other chores were needed.

The next morning we slid our boots into the straps of large hunting snowshoes. Johnny made the frames of birch or willow. Though four and a half feet long, they were light, strong, and artful. The weave was caribou babiche, which Sarah made from dried sinew, sitting for hours carefully splitting it into the proper size with her thumbnail. This she did by feel, rarely looking down at her busy hands.

To stay on top of the extremely dry snow required a tight weave of babiche and a large surface area. Despite the tight weave, the snow crystals readily sifted through and did not accumulate on top of the snowshoe. In wet snow, a smaller snowshoe with a wide weave works well but, still, snow builds up and the snowshoe becomes progressively heavier.

We went upriver a few miles before finding tracks. "Caribou. Fresh tracks, too!" Stanley exclaimed. "You see that little island? Maybe they go in there. You go up this slough." He pointed to the right side of a patch of trees rising between dry, snow-covered channels.

"I'll go around that side," Stanley said, swinging his arm in a large arc. "I'll meet you at the other end. Be ready, caribou might come out."

Stanley traveled fast. By the time we circled the island, he had gone twice the distance I had. The caribou were gone. We ate lunch back in the tent.

"Better if we go back," Stanley said. "Johnny just wanted us to set up camp for him."

It began to snow. He started the snow machine after preheating the engine using a Coleman stove and a couple sections of pipe. As we moved downriver once again I clung to the toboggan handles, wondering why they were made so short. Suddenly two caribou sailed across the trail in front of us and quickly vanished into the trees. There was no time to pull out the rifles, let alone fire. In the falling snow the graceful animals had a dreamlike quality, seeming to float effortlessly through deep drifts.

"Can we follow them?"

"No use. They go too fast for us."

Back at the cabin, Johnny was in a storytelling mood. Between eating, stoking the wood stove, and taking naps, he talked more of his own life experiences.

"1897. That's first time I kill moose, borrow rifle, .44 caliber Winchester. First time I go to Fort Yukon. First time I see steamboat, too.

"1896, lots of gold in Dawson, like gravel—Nome, Coldfoot, too. I never went. Well, when gold is gone in Dawson or everybody got claim, lots men want to go to Nome, go first, go in hurry.

"All winter, no trail. Lots of snow and big wind, too. Everyday trail is gone, covered. They make new trail every day, that wide." Johnny holds his hands about a yard apart. "In first two months, he come down with lots of Indians. You know that? Sometimes man got nothing. Wintertime, some just walk; in summer, use boat. Want to get to Nome, make stake. Dog team? But dog about five hundred dollars that time. Got to watch you dog, too. Watch everything. Some man steal anything. Just walking, no gun, no blanket, nothing. Sometime maybe lots dead men in Yukon along one side of trail." Johnny smoked his pipe, looking quietly at the floor, thinking, picturing this again in memory.

"Lots of white people at Fort Yukon at that time?" I asked.

"Well, most men just go on by it, pass by, keep going. But some men got money and go in store. Big store in Fort Yukon; Canadians start it. All day long store just full. At Circle, too, big store. Used to be big mine there. I remember that store man, Jack McQuesten, big man. He got steamboat, big store. One thing, he help Indian, he like Indian. Marry Indian woman, too.

"I think 1904, I go down to Yukon River. My brother-in-law, Johnny John, got camp there. I go to net fish. Johnny got fifty cords of wood ready to sell. Steamboat land there.

"One big fellow, by golly, come up to me and say, 'You know Jack McQuesten?'

"Yes, one time he stopped in Fort Yukon. At Circle he got mine, big store, steamboat. Sure, I know him. Good man.

"'That's my brother!' He laughed and shook my hand." Johnny chuckled.

"Steamboats burned lots of cord wood, huh?" I asked.

"Every bend, I don't know how many hundreds of cords lined up. Lots of steamboats. Sometimes three or four steamboats go up Yukon when springtime comes."

"Who were the pilots? They'd have to know the river well."

"He want any kind of Indian to be pilot. Some is good man but some don't savvy."

"You ever do that?"

"Me? No! I never work for white people, no. Lots of people do that all time, dog team, too. Me, I go hunt, do little trapping, I get a little fur all the time. I don't worry for anything."

We sat in silence. Dishes rattled as Sarah washed.

"Remember, I tell you. 1897, that's first time I kill moose. Other side of Crow Nest

Mountain, below Arctic Village, there is big mountain. Second big rock is called Crow Nest. Cow moose stand up on other side. I aim long time. That's first time I shoot rifle. Before I shot muzzle-loaded shotgun.

"When the Canadians first come, flour, sugar, *lidii* (tea), tobacco, that's all trade goods they got. Sometime later got muzzle-loaded shotgun. That muzzle-loaded, double barrel, ninety marten skins; single shot, forty-five marten. Shotgun only, no rifle. That time lots of marten. Make a deadfall—no steel trap that time.

"Used to be lots of Indian people go to Barter Island. Before white man, too. Sometimes they got sheep, wolf, wolverine, good fur, too. Eskimo got lots of stuff, see? Trade with Eskimo. Sometime later, start to come the rifle. Expedition company, lots of ships, hunt whale. Lots of stuff. Seven dollar, new rifle."

"You ever go there?"

"No. My father never go up, too. My father lived over by Middle Fork. That's *Di'haii Gwich'in*. Arctic Village is *Netsaii Gwich'in*, talk little bit different. Some Old Crow people are *Di'haii Gwich'in*, too.

"That time man is strong. Strong man, by golly. Run long ways, too. No tired. Sometimes (bands of) people come together. They scared. Lots trouble, see. Long time ago used to be trouble, see? Maybe war. One side stay over here. Other one over there. One man go out from each side, talk together. Not chief but somebody that talk good, make 'em laugh. They tell story, josh each other. If those two men get along, go to one side, talk more. Well, lots of men long time ago talk good. He tell 'em how many travelers come up there, how many go this way; he tell 'em everything there. If they like it, by and by the head guy says, 'Okay. I think it be okay.'

"Everybody come together. By and by, got friends. Dance, every day. Maybe stay one day, maybe one week. If get along good and got food, maybe one month. Sometime when they leave, somebody from one side stay with other. Travel, hunt, learn their story."

Johnny sat back for a while, then leaned forward. "My grandfather, *Ditsii Giitl'uu,* strong man, too. Take bear by neck—just hold bear up. Bear get mad, holler; can't do nothing! Strong man!" Johnny laughed heartily.

"When did first white man come?"

"Well, nobody mark it see? We don't know calendar."

"When did people start to drink?"

"Start drink? 18 ... 1896, 95—something. Cheap, too. One big saloon at Circle. That time no wine, just whiskey. Lots of different whiskey, some strong. Dollar a quart; something like fifty cents for some. Me, I never drink. No good."

"How did those Canadians come up the first time, by boat?"

"No, just walk up. You see Whitehorse? You know big lake? Well, on this side the lake is bad water, white water. Big boat all right and lots of people got poles, paddles. Try to go down. Big river, water sometimes like that," Johnny throws his hands upward and twists.

"Lots of rocks. Try to go down. Boat all broke up, find sticks, that's all. Never find one man. One medicine man watch for long time and figure out how to go. He pilot boat then and go down all right."

"Did the first Canadians come in your grandfather's time?"

"Yeah. My grandfather, he's man that time."

ARCHDEACON HUDSON STUCK, an Episcopal missionary who came to Alaska in 1904, wrote of the terrible effect the gold rush had on Native peoples in his book, *Voyages on the Yukon and its Tributaries,* published by Charles Scribner's Sons in 1917:

> *The great stampede to the Klondike of 1897 and 1898 brought nothing but harm to the native people of Alaska and to those of Fort Yukon in particular. The navigation season of 1897 came to a close with many steamboats far short of their destination. Boats of a draught too great for the shallow waters of the Flats, tied up for the winter at this place, and Captain Ray, of the U.S. Army, who was sent with Lieutenant Richardson to investigate conditions, reports 350 white men wintering at Fort Yukon and is not at all complimentary in his references to the character of many of them. At one time he had to seize merchandise left here en route to Dawson, in the name of the United States, to prevent the looting of it. These were the days when there was no government at all in Alaska. Although the country had been for thirty years in the possession of the United States, our inelastic system had not permitted the setting up of any attempt at governing the Territory.*
>
> *No extraordinary insight is necessary to realize the situation during that winter and the next. Given a large number of white men with little or nothing to do, quantities of whiskey (and there were quantities, though at that time its importation into Alaska was nominally forbidden) and a timid and docile native people, it is not surprising that there was gross debauchery and general demoralization. It took Fort Yukon a long time to recover from the evil living of those winters and the evil name that followed.*

CHAPTER 18

Recording Johnny

For years I thought about preserving Johnny's stories and memories of hunting, endurance, and times of hardship as well as the rich mythology of his people. We discussed this on several occasions. Aware that he was one of the last living repositories of Gwich'in history, Johnny agreed that a book would be good. In the past I had contacted Tanana Chiefs Conference and the University of Alaska in Fairbanks, hoping to find a professional to interview him. But I found no one. I had recorded Johnny just once, in 1967.

"Johnny, should I bring a recorder next time I come?" I had asked during a winter visit.

"Sure." He replied without hesitation. "I'll tell you lots of good stories."

I was overwhelmingly busy at the medical center in 1976. We could have easily kept three orthopedists busy, but I was still the only one. Fortunately there were two orthopedic residents. I desperately needed a week off and arranged for a colleague in private practice to cover emergencies. No elective surgery was scheduled. In September I headed north.

In Venetie I stayed with Walter John, an elder. We spent the evening talking.

"How are you going to Gold Camp, fly?" he asked.

"No, I'll walk." I motioned to my pack and rifle.

"Who is going with you?"

"Just me. I haven't walked it in fourteen years."

"The trail is pretty brushy, I hear. Nobody walks it anymore, just go by snow machine in winter."

He lifted my pack, "What the heck you got in here?"

I laughed, "There are a couple of large lantern batteries, a tape recorder, and about ten tapes in addition to my stuff."

"You going to get Johnny Frank's stories?"

"Well, I hope so. Need to save them."

"Good. That old man knows lots of stories."

By the time I got to Big Lake, only three miles, I had a blister on each foot. My boots were broken in but I had put on an extra pair of socks. The tundra and taiga forest floor was soft but dry. After I waded the short cut around the lake, I removed my boots and socks to assess the situation. Maggie Roberts had just given me a beautiful pair of beaded moose-skin moccasins. I had planned to wear them only in camp but I decided to put them on over a fresh pair of socks. After all, it was the footgear used here for thousands of years, beads replacing dyed porcupine quills. The moccasins were light and soft. I had no further trouble with my feet.

I walked well into the deep twilight of night. Suddenly, tired and barely able to see in the poor light, I convinced myself that there was a bear in the trail ahead. I imagined it moved and brought my rifle to a ready position. For long minutes I stood still, squinting, feeling my heart thumping in my chest. Memories of a cold winter morning in South Carolina returned to me. I was ten or eleven and crossing a meadow alone in predawn light, clutching my shotgun, on my way to a slough for duck hunting. There had been accounts of a mysterious predator killing sheep in North Carolina. As I approached the edge of the woods, I abruptly stopped at the sight of a dark form. I was sure it was an animal and came close to shooting it indiscriminately. My training had been good—never shoot at anything unless you are sure what it is, I was told. I waited, my heart in my throat, expecting an attack. As the sun rose, daylight revealed a bush.

My mind returned to the present. Dawn was several hours away. The bear was in the trail. I preferred not to walk through the thick forest to get around it. Slowly, I crept forward with the .30-.30 ready. Another bush! In an adrenaline tremor, I laughed at myself, glad to be alone.

The next afternoon I stood at the river's edge across from Gold Camp. Large holes had worn through my moccasins. It must have been quite a task to keep a family in footwear in the old days. The weather was good. It was early September, the height of fall in the Arctic, and bearberry and cranberry covered the ground in bright red splotches, contrasting with golden leaves of the birch and willow. There were no bothersome insects. I made a fire and piled on green spruce boughs. A thick column of smoke rose into the air. I shot my rifle several times and lay back on a bed of deep dry moss. It felt good repeating this walk, even though the mountaintops were more brushy with hip-high bushes in places where it had been mid-calf high in 1962.

Eventually Johnny appeared alone on the opposite bank with a canvas canoe. He gave a big wave. By then Johnny was in his late nineties; some believed he was more than one hundred years old. He carefully placed the boat along the shore, balanced it with a paddle across the gunnels, and stepped into the frail craft. The boat hit the main current and floated rapidly downstream but Johnny ferried across without a problem, landing below me. After a warm greeting we carried the boat upstream and crossed back over to the camp.

At Gold Camp, Maggie and her husband, Jimmy Roberts, stood with her mother Sarah on the bank outside the cabin. Several of their children laughed and squealed as they ran about. Not many visitors came here. Those who did usually arrived by airplane or motorboat.

Later we sat in the cabin discussing how to record Johnny. "How we do this?" he asked. "In my language? Who is going to fix it?"

"Say it in your language, and we will get someone to translate it later... maybe Lawrence, Robert or Eddie John. What do you think?"

"Well, right now all Indians don't savvy old peoples' language ... pretty hard."

"How about Jessie?"

"I tried Jessie, but she don't savvy old words."

"Well, I'll try it. Good story, old lady and fish!" he laughed. "Fix it." He pointed to the recorder. Maggie hushed the children and told them to be quiet while Grandpa talked. Johnny started to tell a story in Gwich'in without hesitation. Then he said, "No good. You don't understand."

During the week the remainder of seven hours of taping was in English. Many of the stories I had heard but had forgotten various details. I noticed that Johnny usually wasn't using 'she' when he meant 'he,' as he had years before, though some of the stories were still hard to follow. At first I tried to guide the process. Sarah, Maggie, and the children listened. The children were cooperative.

"Did you start the reservation?" I asked.

"Yeah, me and John Fredson. One time government man tell me, 'Give up that reservation, too big.' Well, I listen. Then I tell him good. 'Good for trap line, this ground. Little gold, silver, oil—everything. Lots of fish. I put net in Yukon. Lots of animals, too. That's why I need it.

"'This is my homestead!' That's what I tell him. I want to say, 'Money is your god! If you got foxy (smart like a fox) you don't need money. Just use caribou, moose, and rabbit. If you got no foxy, sure, you need it!" Johnny laughed. "Eskimo, Indian are stockholders of the land. Me, the land! Lose that money quick."

I wanted to know more about how the Venetie Indian Reservation was established but he began talking about his family.

"My mother's father, my father's father, too—big chiefs. I remember my grandmother; she about three or four years old when lots of people starving. All over nothing, no animals. Big bunch of people stay together. How many people there I don't know. Some people go one way. One family go other way. Try to find food.

"Well, one man go out, his wife too. Got one kid, no dog. That man and old lady put up skin tent. They got three or four caribou skin. Make camp. Big pile of snow right there. They make fire this side. Everybody sleep. Long time, never eat. Little boy can't do nothing; he's too weak. Next morning boy smell something burn. Smell like fingernail (hoof), moose fingernail. He smell it. He tell his mother but she all (done) in. His father, too, can't get up. Well, that kid two or three time say 'I smell something like fingernail burn.'

"That man tell his wife, 'That kid smell something. You look around fire.'

"Big bull moose foot right there. Fire melt snow, see?

"'Don't worry, my husband, that kid no lie. Big bull foot, burn fingernail right there.'

"That big pile of snow, two big bull moose, by golly." Johnny laughs. "In fall time those big bulls fight, lock horn. Can't get free. Just die right there. Snow cover and make big pile. When leg got little warm, man take little meat, all three, just a bite. That fire melt snow and free leg. Then man take the skin off. Anything, even bite might make 'em throw up, see? Their stomach just like nothing—no belly. Never eat long time." Johnny rested back on the bed, smoking his ever-present pipe, thinking. "Strong life, that time!"

Sarah was sitting on the bed, her feet doubled under her, dish towel in her hard-worked hands. "Hard time. Hard time, that time," she mused.

"Well, they made big fire, melt snow, keep warm but don't sleep. Lots of fat, good meat, too—just take little bite.

"That man take meat, fat and go, find family. Give 'em bite. Boy eat. That boy go to another family, give 'em food. Then another family, all around. All night, keep at it. Two, three, four bites; every man not strong, see? Never sleep, just keep going. Save lot of people. That's what lots of people say."

A CESSNA 185 buzzed the cabin. We went out as it circled the valley, then lined up to land on the gravel-bar strip. It bumped to a stop and two men got out.

"Who is that, Johnny?" I asked.

"Funny, new plane. I don't know."

I took the boat across to meet them. "Ernie Vent," the white man introduced himself. "You probably know Noah," he nodded toward his Native companion. "I'm staying up on Wind River, trapping." We shook hands and I took them across.

"Hi, Johnny, Sarah. I brought you some sheep meat," Ernie said.

"Neenjit doonch'yaa? Gwinzii, gwinzii. I'm glad to see you. Come, have tea." Sarah was already filling the kettle. She placed it on the oil-drum stove, still outside for the summer.

"You see any moose when you come over?" Johnny asked.

"Nothing," Noah answered.

The kids gathered around to watch Grandma Sarah take care of the fresh sheep quarter. Johnny and Noah spoke to one another in Gwich'in. Maggie helped Sarah. Ernie had been in the Wind River country for two years, living by himself. He trapped with Christian Tritt. Ernie was generous to the locals. Maggie's husband wanted to go to Venetie, so Ernie flew him over and returned with mail. Johnny and Sarah had checks. We got a good laugh when Johnny signed both of them. They got a small but regular longevity bonus from the state.

The visitors stayed a couple of hours. Johnny and Noah seemed to enjoy one another's company. After they left, Johnny became unusually quiet and remained so throughout the evening. He seemed pensive so we left him alone. After a while he went outside.

Johnny returned an hour later, dripping wet from a light rain. Sarah and I were eating sheep soup, a favorite of Johnny's, but he did not join us. Eventually, as he stirred sugar into a cup of tea, he said, "That's best man, Noah. Best man but too much he likes to drink. Too bad. Well, I tell him, 'You stop here. Stay at Gold Camp.' Lots of time I tell him."

The children talked in low voices with Sarah in Gwich'in. She held their hands in hers, one by one, and gently responded. Their language carried well at low volume. I wondered if this was an adaptation to living in small spaces as well as using tones that would not tend to frighten animals.

"Noah ever stop here?" I asked.

"No. He say he want to go on trap line. I tell him, 'I got good trap line. One place lots of marten; one place lots of wolverine. We can go to Ackerman Lake ... straight trail.' I got lots of tents, traps, shells ... .30-.30, .30-.06, shotgun.

"Well, he say he want to go but no time. No time! He go to Fort Yukon, Fairbanks drinking all the time, like that. He find out now that he is almost blind.

"Me, I'm stakeholder in Alaska. Every Eskimo or Indian is stakeholder in Alaska. Lose money quick. The land, the land! We need it!"

THE NEXT MORNING, Johnny told another story about *Naa'in,* the bush man.

"Paul Solomon's father's sister ... you know Paul Solomon?" Paul was a Gwich'in elder who lived in Fort Yukon. "Paul Solomon's father stop down at fish camp. Well, that girl stop over on Chandalar. In fall time she want to go down to fish camp but only a little snow. She come down anyway but pretty hard travel. At that time no trail to Fort Yukon, just follow the river, see? *Naa'in* all time stay at this big mountain. Well, when she go down, there's little snow on ice so *Naa'in* see tracks; he catch her and take her up to his house."

Johnny sat back. He was quiet and seemed to be through with his story.

I was confused. "That sister?"

"Aaha.

"Well, *Naa'in* steal that girl and they have big family. After he get old and die, she stay up there. They don't like village, have good place on mountain. That's better. No trouble, no hungry."

"How did they get food?" Bush men remained a mystery to me. Sometimes they seemed to be outcasts or hermits. In other stories they were magical.

"Arrow. Just use bow and arrow. Never miss one time. In the ground he got a hole. Way down in ground is the house. Big house, too. On one side, big pile of wood." Johnny demonstrated with his hands. "Other side, big warehouse ... dry meat, fat, everything. He got lots of wood. When he make a fire, lots of smoke come up. He make smoke go away. He got big fire but no smoke!" Johnny laughed.

Silent for moments, he sat puffing his pipe. "Sometime *Naa'in* kill lots of caribou. He cut off all meat. Well, he holler, 'Don't ruin that meat!' That's what he holler. Warm place, too. Caribou meat in big pile, never get rotten. Blow fly don't bother, too."

"Does bush man bother people sometime?"

"Yeah. Well ... he go out in woods, I tell you, find good place ... water, wood, everything. He holler. Nothing. He want a hole. He walk little ways and go like this." Johnny made a circular motion downward with his hand. "By golly, big hole (appears), right there. He go inside. Wood, warehouse ..." his voice tapered off again.

I asked, "Some bush men are medicine man, too?"

"Yeah, some of them. Strong, too. Well, even if no medicine, he's best man—can do everything."

"Make skin clothing?" I was determined to know more. Johnny rarely talked about *Naa'in.*

"Yeah."

"Snowshoe, too?"

"Yeah, he got everything. Saw, everything. Make dry meat, grease, fat ... how much you want ... hundred pounds, five hundred pounds ... ."

Johnny ate, boiled dry meat and rice.

"You told me before you dreamed bear so bear can't hurt you?" I asked another time.

"Well, nobody know dream. Anything has got a power. Long time ago, everything comes from the water, see? Everything alive is from the water. Animals, all kind of animals comes from the water. Everything got spirit.

"When you die—if all you life you want anything too much—grub, money, woman, anything, then spirit gets stuck. Can't go up. Never see light. Light, that's God.

"Long time ago we don't know Bible, Jesus, God. We just say 'up'—*'yi'ee dak'* ... just like

God. If some kind of man lie, cheat, steal—then we say 'down' or '*de en den gee.*'

"Every medicine man ... not all of them are good. Some when he dream bear, he want to fight all the time. That's bad one; he want to kill anything.

"Some are doctor. Sometime you get hurt, go to him to fix it. That's all he use power for.

"One time there was a medicine man up East Fork. Well, that time lots of people, too many people. They got no food. Every day they go out. No animals. Somebody ask him to find caribou.

"'Alright,' he says.

"Next day early he go out, make trail. By and by, when daylight, people follow, ladies and all. He tell them, 'You stay right here. Make a fire.' They make big fire. Everybody circle round. 'Use snowshoes and make a snow pile that high.' —" He raises his hand four feet from the floor.

"He start to sing to fire." Johnny sings in Gwich'in. "Two times he walk around fire. Then he go up to snow pile, reach inside." Johnny suddenly reaches forward with both hands and then pulls back, his eyes wide in surprise. Sarah listens intently, her hands still in her lap.

"By golly, he hold cow caribou head! Caribou look at all the people. Just look around. She look in eyes, everything. Shake off snow, move head," Johnny shakes his head and we all laugh at his expression. "'Everybody look, see what kind of caribou. Everybody look already?'

"'Yes!' Everybody say."

Johnny pushes his hands out, as if thrusting the caribou head back into the snow. "Nothing! There is only big snow pile.

"Well, after little daylight come, he tell everybody, 'Make a line fifteen miles long. Stay like that.'"

Johnny makes a straight line with his hand. "Make another line over there, fifteen miles long. Then two lines come together." He sweeps his outstretched arms together.

"They do that and kill lot of caribou."

"Good medicine when used that way," I said.

"Yeah, lot of good doctor, too. Good doctor, never use his power to kill man. Caribou, moose, anything—he dream good. He never kill man."

Johnny rubbed his arms. He'd been splitting wood.

"Sore, huh?"

"Yeah, that nine-pound hammer. Short wood but hard to split."

"*Vasaagihdzak?*" I asked, remembering his first story of *Vasaagihdzak* making twisted trees.

"Yeah, twister. Well, go to bed now. We talk more tomorrow."

"Good stories. Thank you, grandfather."

"*Aaha.* Goodnight, grandson."

Johnny was making a fire in the barrel stove when I awoke. The fresh smell of spruce burning filled the cabin. When Johnny saw that I was awake, he smiled and said, "Good morning, grandson, you sleep good?"

I nodded, "Yes, Johnny. You?"

"Sleep good! I make coffee."

As we drank coffee, he said, as he frequently did, "Just drink one cup coffee, then just *lidii, lidii* all day. *Lidii,* that's my wine." Johnny laughed. "Feel good this morning."

I STOOD WITH Johnny on the bank overlooking the old Venetie village site, which was subject to flooding. Now everyone lived up on top of the bluff, farther from the river. It was July 1977. The Arctic mid-summer sunset lasted hours as the sun traversed the northern sky in a low arc. The lowest point indicated north. It would be highest in the south at noon.

A young boy drove a three-wheeler around and around the few village roads. It was irritating and I resisted an urge to stop him. Seldom was it quiet in Venetie now. Johnny shook his head, clenching a cold pipe in his few remaining teeth. He did not smile as he removed his pipe. The boy represented much change in village life. His activity was useless, frivolous, wasteful, and bothersome.

"No good." Johnny shook his head again as he carefully filled the curved pipe with his blend of Granger and chipped Black Bull tobaccos.

After quietly watching the large golden clouds awhile, Johnny said, "One time Henry John was standing here. Good medicine man. Well, he feel something. Maybe somebody try to kill him, see? Just go out, spirit." Johnny swept his left arm out with little fluttering clicks of the fingers against his thumb, indicating Henry's spirit went out from the bank down over the river. "Well, he find two Eskimo way down. Medicine men, too, asleep by fire. Well, he kill 'em right there. Never wake up."

Johnny rarely spoke of any recent medicine events. "Maybe they hear Henry is strong medicine man. Try to kill him."

I had heard similar stories from Johnny. A medicine man would feel some presence and go out to meet it alone, face to face with another medicine man who had come to "try" him. Across a gravel bar they might face one another until one gave way to the other's power or presence. There was no physical struggle, yet one would leave in defeat or die.

After a moment of silence, Johnny turned toward me, "Too old. Eye, teeth, ears no good. Pretty soon maybe die. That'll be okay. Now I'm ready." I was grateful for his long life and the effect he and Sarah had on my life. When we first met in 1961, Johnny said he was eighty-one. That would make him about ninety-seven now. He'd vowed to live to be one hundred.

"Then I die, that's okay," he'd said at the time, laughing.

For a while we stood quietly watching the clouds change shape, bathed in golden and red hues. Then he turned to me and, knowing my temper, advised, "Just you remember, don't get mad, no use."

We walked back to the little house where he and Sarah were crowded into a small room. Surrounded by unfinished wallboard, lighted by a single light bulb dangling on a cord, Sarah half reclined on a mattress on the floor. I sat next to her and she held my hands.

Johnny's talk of death prompted me to now ask, "When somebody dies, what do you think happens to their spirit?"

At first I thought he'd not understood my question. After a moment or two, he said seriously, "Well, spirit go out somewhere, never die." Another silence. "Before I was born, I lived in northern lights four years. I was boss, too. Lots of kinds of animals lived there. Every kind. I tell 'em do something, they do it. Just like I'm energy—just bright light. Below, nothing. I look around.

"Maybe sometime good man come back again, so he find woman and want to be baby, some get born. That's all."

Sarah leaned forward, listening, gently twisting a scarf in her beautiful, well-used, gentle hands. Johnny continued, "That's why all animals like me. Never scared. Me, I'm little bit scared sometimes when I was young. Animal come close and look at me. Never bother me, too.

"One time in northern lights there were lots of big men. Everything was flat like big sheet, like plywood or maybe ice, just smooth. All together, just dance. Everybody dance. Well, something come up, walk on water, like glass. Something evil, like giant." Something in Johnny's expression gave me the impression of a threatening, dark presence. "Maybe that's devil. Nobody know. Come up. Walk like that. Johnny held one arm crooked across his chest. "Anything that touch him just die. He come up in front. I tell him, 'Stop there! You don't bother us. You come close, I kill you.'"

Johnny explained that he and the evil giant had faced each other across broken ice pads on which they stood as if on a large frozen sea. "Well, he keep coming. We fight. Ice move. Finally I catch him by chest and throw him down. He go down deep in water. Lots waves, strong sea," he indicated with both arms a violent rocking motion. "I almost fall, too. After he disappear, everything get calm again. Settle down, just smooth. He never bother again. That's why, too, nobody ever bother me. Animal see me, they know me."

I was astonished. Johnny had never said anything like this to me. I hardly knew how to respond but needed to know more. Usually I waited patiently with quiet interest for him to say more.

"So you were like a good spirit fighting bad?"

"*Aaha,*" he replied. "Pretty soon after that I'm born."

We sat wrapped in silence and thought.

I left the next morning. We looked into one another's eyes as we said goodbye; I felt it was for the last time.

"*Shanandaii,* you remember for me."

"*Neenahaldiia,* I remember for you."

CHAPTER 19

Volunteer Lobbyist

B ack at the Alaska Native Medical Center, I had to hold on for only one more month. In September, Bill Paton arrived, expecting to be our third orthopedist. Rick Garner had come on the ortho staff the previous November. When I sustained a herniated disk in my lower back, Rick graciously took over as department chief. I was burned out emotionally and physically. I wanted a break from medicine. I resigned my Public Health Service commission, planning to return in January to work eight months a year under a more flexible civil-service arrangement.

I spent much of the fall of 1977 in Washington, D.C. as a volunteer lobbyist supporting rural subsistence hunting and fishing priority in the so-called "d-2" bill, House Resolution 39, introduced by Representative Morris Udall of Arizona. HR 39 was an offshoot of the Alaska Native Claims Settlement Act (ANCSA) passed in 1971. Section 17 d-2 of ANCSA mandated that the secretary of the interior review federal lands in Alaska and recommend up to eighty million acres to Congress for protection as new federal parks, wildlife refuges, and other conservation units. ANCSA terminated aboriginal hunting and fishing rights but a Congressional report acknowledged the need for a preference to be given to those dependent on fish and wildlife for survival. About two-thirds of the food in many rural villages comes from the land or the sea. Jobs that paid cash were limited and usually seasonal, such as firefighting or construction.

I represented the Alaska Chapter of the Sierra Club, having been a member of the organization's state executive committee for four years. The Sierra Club worked with many other conservation organizations and the legislative House Interior Subcommittee staff in preparing and supporting the passage of HR 39. Most of this was done on a national level but the Alaska Chapter took on drafting a section dealing with the subsistence issue. We had encouraged Native involvement in our work, but with little success, and the subsistence section became controversial when the bill was introduced. Native leaders believed they had not been consulted. Guides and sport hunters opposed any type of subsistence preference for rural villagers. It was an intense, emotional issue.

Meanwhile, the International Whaling Commission had declared a moratorium on Native subsistence hunting of bowhead whales, expressing alarm at an increasing take of bowheads and the rising number of struck and lost whales. The IWC considered the bowhead population to be threatened. Inuit hunters believed the bowhead population actually was increasing. The whales had come close to extinction due to commercial whaling in the 1890s and early 1900s.

I conducted orthopedic clinics in Barrow four times a year and had met many of the whalers in this largest Inuit town in Alaska. In the evenings I visited the homes of older whaling captains where I observed preparations for whaling. Women gathered to sew waterproof seams in the heavy, tough bearded seal hides that covered the umiat boat frames.

I sensed the deep individual and community need to hunt the whales. For hundreds of years Inuit whaling crews had gone out on the sea ice, waiting for the whales to appear in open water. To launch a skin-covered boat and paddle through icy water toward an animal over twice the length of the frail craft took great courage and teamwork among the crews. The hunts brought everyone together. The entire community was involved in pulling the whale out of the water, and the butchering and distribution of the blubber and meat. Boat captains were highly respected, especially those who landed whales. These men had a great social and economic responsibility. They paid for all equipment and expenses for the camps. They had to direct their crew safely. They provided food for everyone and put on large seasonal community festivals.

I strongly supported Inuit whaling, but became aware of a growing problem among the whalers. Normally it took years to acquire the skills and financial means to become a whaling captain. This was changing as young men returned with cash from high-paying construction jobs on the trans-Alaska oil pipeline. Rather than serving years of apprenticeship, the younger generation was having boats and equipment made and forming their own crews of young men who operated free of the strict traditional Inuit boating hierarchy.

A senior whaling captain had expressed to me his growing concern. Sitting forward in his chair, he spoke with his lower jaw thrust forward. "Doctor, these young men are not ready to be a boat captain but they come back with ten thousand dollars and pay to get everything. Always the whaling captains have been in control but now they don't listen to us. They make too many struck and lost whales. They don't even know which side to approach the whale, so there's danger, too."

I was torn between the need to allow Native whaling and an uneasy feeling that the hunting was getting out of traditional control. Our Sierra Club chapter supported a limited take in opposition to the position of the national organization, which supported the moratorium, as did most other national environmental groups. An exception was Friends of the Earth.

On arrival in D.C., I went to the Sierra Club office to help with lobbying efforts on HR 39 and was informed by the senior staff that it had the work covered. They did not need me. I left feeling dismayed and walked to the Friends of the Earth office, where Alaskans Cathy Smith and Pam Rich shared a desk in a crowded attic room. They had moved to the capital to work full time for the passage of HR 39. In half an hour Pam laid out a month's worth of work and arranged for me to accompany Steve Young of the National Audubon Society to the House of Representatives to learn how to lobby.

My spirit was restored. The attic desk became my base and guidance center. It also put me in the center of the whaling controversy among national environmental groups. Pam and Cathy were catching hell for FOE's support of the Native whalers. Thirty to forty representatives of environmental and animal-rights groups met several times a week. After several emotionally charged gatherings, Pam and Cathy were forbidden to attend the meetings.

ONE AFTERNOON I sat on the small lawn in front of FOE's office in an old frame building as Chip Brown, an independent journalist, interviewed Charlie Edwardsen, Jr. Charlie was chairman of the recently organized Alaska Eskimo Whaling Commission.

Chip asked, "Charlie, what is your feeling about the environmental groups?"

Charlie looked up and said, "FOE is our only friend in a sea of shit!"

A WEEK LATER, I went to The Wilderness Society headquarters with Jim Kowalsky, Alaska representative of Friends of the Earth, for a private showing of a film by John Denver. It featured Denver's recent trip to Alaska lauding the white hippie "return to the land" movement and lamenting the "loss" of Native culture. The film, which Denver hoped to get on national television, supported the whaling moratorium. I lost my temper and swore to Denver that I would do everything I could to oppose a national viewing of his film unless he reversed his position on Native whaling.

I was still steaming when a man in a tailored suit joined Jim and me in the elevator. As the door closed, he asked, "Tell me, are the Eskimos still machine-gunning caribou?"

Again I responded in anger. "There was a well-publicized incident of a few young boys from Kotzebue slaughtering a lot of caribou and leaving them to rot. Natives and whites alike deplored this wanton waste and disregard for life. To judge all Natives by the action of a few is prejudiced."

We went opposite ways outside. "Guess you know that was Larry Rockefeller," Jim said.

I didn't know the wealthy conservationist and didn't care.

I became convinced that a meeting between environmentalists and members of the Alaska Eskimo Whaling Commission would clear up a lot of misunderstanding about the whaling issue. Once the whaling captains expressed reasons for their belief that the bowhead population was increasing and explained their peoples' deep spiritual connection to the whales, I expected that the environmental community would support a limited take under the direction of the Eskimo whaling commission. I pleaded with both groups to come together to discuss the issue.

Finally we gathered in an oak-paneled room in the office of the Washington law firm representing the Eskimo whalers. Charlie Edwardsen Jr. was absent. Craig Van Note, executive director of Monitor, a coalition of animal-rights' groups, tried to get the meeting started without Edwardsen. The Inuit sat silently awaiting the arrival of their spokesperson. I nodded a greeting to Arnold Brower Sr., a community leader and well-respected whaling captain. For half an hour we sat waiting in the crowded conference room. One of the lawyers for the whaling commission took the opportunity to berate the environmentalists for supporting the moratorium. The environmentalists remained calm.

Finally Charlie arrived, weaving drunkenly, his suit a mess. He looked as if he had slept in a gutter. I was stunned. He surveyed the group before speaking, his face full of fury. Then he began explosively began, "You fucking people!"

Charlie ranted and raved. The whaling captains were silent. When Craig Van Note asked if we could hear from other members of the whaling commission, Charlie exploded. "I represent them! I'm the chairman! They elected me to speak for them!"

The meeting was over. I felt sick. We milled about and there was little talking. A few people spoke to me but I could think of nothing intelligent to say. Gradually people left. I went back to FOE and reported to Pam and Cathy.

"I'm leaving tonight," I told them. "There is no need for me to be here. There will be no understanding now. It was terrible."

Pam and Cathy urged me to stay for two more days to join them at a meeting with the Eskimo whalers. Celia Hunter from The Wilderness Society and Dave Cline of the National Audubon Society also would attend.

My wife and son were visiting her parents on Long Island. Reluctantly I phoned. "Liz, I need to stay in D.C. a few more days for a meeting."

"Again? When are you going to leave there? This is the third time you have postponed coming here."

"I'm sorry but I need to do this."

The meeting was incredible. Charlie Edwardsen was sober and charming. The whalers were relaxed and told personal stories about their experiences. This was what the other environmental and animal-rights people should have heard. I realized that Charlie had been elected to head the Alaska Eskimo Whaling Commission because he expressed the collective anger of the gathered elders, who could not bring themselves to display anger in public.

An emergency International Whaling Commission meeting was held in Japan in December. The moratorium was rescinded. The Eskimos received a quota of fourteen whales or eighteen "strikes" under control of the Alaska Eskimo Whaling Commission. Joint research conducted by the Eskimo commission and scientists eventually showed that the bowhead population was larger than originally estimated by the scientific community, and was in fact increasing.

CHAPTER 20

Bad News

In November that year the snow lay deep on the road to my cabin on a mountain slope east of Anchorage. Not expecting visitors, I was startled by the sound of foot stomping and a knock on the door.

"Come in! Come in." I called, rising from my chair. Bill Paton entered the arctic entry, brushing off snow.

"Welcome! To what do I owe this visit?"

"Bad news, I'm afraid. Johnny Frank had a stroke and is in Fairbanks Memorial Hospital. He is evidently in a coma. A family member called the hospital today to let you know. We have been busy at the hospital, and there was no way to call you, but I came as soon as I could."

I thanked Bill for coming all the way out to the cabin. I'd given up the radiophone when I quit working at the hospital.

The next morning David and I stood by the roadside in Fairbanks with our thumbs out. Only his eyes were visible between his marten hat and scarf. We had taken the early-morning flight to Fairbanks. It was twenty-five below.

A Mercedes sedan pulled over, to my surprise. As we climbed in, the driver asked, "Where are you going?"

"Memorial Hospital. Thanks for stopping."

"Visiting a friend?"

"Yes, an elder, my son's godfather had a stroke."

At the hospital, family sat around Johnny's bed quietly conversing in Gwich'in. I went to Sarah. She took my hand as I pressed my face to hers. "*Mahsi' choo,* grandson, I'm glad to see you, you son, too!" She gave David a hug.

Johnny looked small and dark against the white sheets. His eyes were shut, his mouth open, and his face turned to the right. I took his hand and spoke to him, "Hello, Grandpa Johnny, this is Mike Holloway. David and I are here. Sarah, Maggie, and your family are here with you. You had a stroke and are in the hospital at Fairbanks."

Commonly hospital staff and even family talked about an unresponsive patient but rarely to them. I believed that often the person could understand at some level even if unable to respond.

After a round of greetings, Maggie said, "Tuesday he had a stroke but could still walk. They sent a plane. When he got here, he had another stroke and has been like this."

Johnny always enjoyed hymns. The family took turns holding his hand as we sang hymns, talked to him, and visited. Many people came by to give their regards. Sarah also believed Johnny could understand and was aware of our presence. She spoke softly to him in their language.

Dr. Jack Raba stopped by and gave me a review of Johnny's condition. I told him that Johnny had expressed to me his feeling that he was ready to die. No medical heroics were in order. David and I stayed several days. There was no change in Johnny's condition.

ONE EVENING IN early December a friend and I sat by my wood stove, sipping Tennessee whiskey, when someone started up the steps outside. It was Rick Garner, and I knew this was no casual visit. My cabin was twenty-five miles from town. I invited him to join us.

"Well, I came with news you might not like," Rick said. "The orthopedic workload and situation at the hospital require that you come back on staff full-time."

"The agreement we've worked out is for eight months a year beginning in January," I said.

"Yes, but I'm afraid that is not possible. It will be full-time or nothing."

"Nothing, then."

"Not so fast! With three of us, it will be better. Come back full-time."

"No, I am not ready for that."

A WEEK LATER, I attended a small conference in Juneau regarding the subsistence hunting and fishing section of the d-2 bill. During a coffee break I talked with George Allen, who followed subsistence issues for the Rural Alaska Community Action Program, known as "RurAL CAP," a nonprofit organization working to improve the quality of life for low-income Alaskans.

"So, you are going back to the hospital soon?"

"No, that's changed. I was to return part-time, eight months a year. Now they say full-time or nothing, so I chose the latter."

"What are you going to do?"

"Keep on lobbying for a subsistence priority."

"You want to work with RurAL CAP?"

"Full-time?" I asked.

"Yes."

"No, eight months a year," I said.

An hour later George held up ten fingers. I shook my head. A bit later, he held up eight fingers and I nodded acceptance. I would start January 2, 1978, as a "subsistence advocate" and liaison between the villages and Washington, D.C.

A few days after Christmas, I sat in a conference room in Anchorage looking over handouts at a public meeting. It was likely to be contentious as it involved allocation of hunting and fishing rights. The subsistence taking of fish and wildlife to provide food for families and communities would have priority over sport, trophy, or commercial uses.

Someone approached, "Are you Mike Holloway?"

"Yes."

"They said to tell you Johnny Frank died yesterday."

The man quickly disappeared in the crowd before I could respond. I did not know who he was, how he got the message, or who "they" were. I was unable to contact anyone in Venetie. It was Tuesday. Friday, I thought. The funeral will probably be Friday.

Friday morning I flew to Fairbanks and took a cab to the airfield for small planes to catch a commuter flight to Fort Yukon and from there another would get me to Venetie. As I paced the waiting room, a Native man came in and bought a ticket to Fort Yukon. I was wrapped in thoughts of Johnny and did not feel like talking. We were the only two passengers on the eight-passenger plane to Fort Yukon. There we waited until a Cessna 185 arrived and we boarded, again the only passengers. Still we did not talk.

One lone person stood by the airstrip in Venetie. Dennis Eric, a Gwich'in friend married to Maggie's oldest daughter, greeted me, "Drop your pack at Stanley's; then we'll go to the church. Everyone else is already there." The village streets were quiet, deserted.

We pushed into the small log church, packed with people. I went to Sarah. The service began immediately. The four ministers were all Native. The first missionary to Gwich'in country had been Anglican, William Kirby, who arrived at Fort Yukon in 1861. He stayed only one week but arranged for Robert MacDonald, an Ojibwa-Scot, to come the following year. The Anglican Church Missionary Society actively promoted an indigenous ministry, a concept not pursued by other denominations. MacDonald stayed for years, married a Gwich'in woman, and translated the Bible, prayer book, and hymnal into a regional Indian dialect called *Takudh*. His books were still in use. At the church I recognized three of the Native ministers—Paul Tritt of Venetie, David Salmon of Chalkyitsik, and Trimble Gilbert of Arctic Village.

The plywood coffin sat on saw horses within arm's reach. Many older people were there. I was the only white. The service was mostly in Gwich'in, though some letters were read in English. It was announced in both languages that Johnny had been ninety-eight, though some believed he was older; he and Sarah were married for seventy-five years and had fourteen children, of whom only four were living; they also had forty-five to fifty-five grandchildren, some twenty-two great grandchildren; and many others they called grandchildren. Johnny's favorite Gwich'in hymns were sung.

Sorrow and anguish came to me in waves. Johnny had not regained consciousness. The week before Christmas the family informed Doctor Raba that they wanted him to die among his people in Venetie. The doctor accompanied Johnny on a charter flight and helped get him settled. The family appreciated this effort.

The top was lifted from the coffin and set aside. Johnny looked peaceful. Gone was the facial contortion of the stroke. Mourners passed by in a line. Most touched his chest and face. Small children were lifted to see and touch him. His face was cold to my hand. As the church emptied, the lid was replaced. Jimmy Roberts picked up a hammer. Together we carefully aligned the top. I held it in place as Jimmy nailed. The hammer blows resonated loudly in the small church. Young men raised the coffin to their shoulders. I followed as they carried Johnny up the hill to the graveyard at the end of the airstrip. A few other whites attended the brief graveside service. The grave was a perfect rectangle seven or eight feet deep with sharply cut walls. Digging it had been quite a feat given that it had been forty to fifty below since Johnny's death. I learned later that the gravediggers had thawed the concrete-hard ground little by little burning diesel fuel, and that the extra depth was a sign of respect.

The coffin was placed over the grave on boards and ropes passed under it. It was lifted, the boards were removed, and the coffin was lowered by hand. Several men took up picks and shovels to loosen the large pile of frozen earth nearby and began to fill in the grave. Dirt struck loudly on the coffin at first, becoming muffled as it filled. Turns were taken with the four or five shovels. Hesitant at first, I took a shovel and began to help. I was closer to Johnny than many here. I was astonished. This work brought sudden and unexpected relief. Never before had I taken such a direct part in a funeral. In Western society we were separated from this. The sadness remained but the anguish was gone. I worked until I was sweating before relinquishing the shovel.

Grandma Sarah and many others were staying at Stanley's cabin so I moved my pack to Silas John's and returned to Stanley's. People streamed in and out, laughing, talking and eating. Sarah was calm and serene, holding hands, smiling, reassuring people as she sat on the bed. She motioned for me to join her and made space at her side. She introduced me to Hannah Solomon, daughter of Lucy Frank, Sarah's first born, and Ambrose Williams. Then she asked Hannah to translate.

After Sarah spoke at length, Hannah gave a brief translation. When this was repeated the next time she spoke, Sarah spoke firmly to Hannah, who lowered her head. Sarah started again and this time Hannah's translation was detailed. As Sarah held my hand, she told me about Johnny's last days at Gold Camp in November.

"On a Friday Johnny sat at the table drinking tea and smoking his pipe. He turned and said he was seeing some kind of light in his vision and had a noise in his head. He lay back on the bed and was unconscious for a while. When he came to, he was able to move and walk, but felt tired, and rested in bed the next few days. Charlie Laughlin flew out from Fairbanks to see us on the weekend. He has a small airplane and brought us groceries, and visited sometimes. He wanted to take Johnny back to Fairbanks for a checkup but Johnny would not go.

"On Sunday Johnny split wood. I told him not to do it but that old man never listen," Sarah chuckled. "The next morning he woke early and cooked a large breakfast. Usually he didn't eat much anymore. That morning he ate three fried eggs, meat, coffee and tea. He sat back, filled his pipe, and tried to light it but he couldn't strike that wooden match. 'That's funny,' he said, 'I can't strike it!' He got me to do it.

"'I can't feel the pipe in my mouth,' he said. 'My right hand, too, I can't feel it.' Then he heard a noise in his head again. He said it was not a roar but more like 'eeeeeeee-eeeeeee'nn,'" Sarah mimicked. "He said, 'Jesus coming, Jesus coming!' and lay back on the bed against the blankets and passed out again. When he woke up his right arm and leg were weak. By Tuesday he could get around a little. Then Hilda, that nurse from Fort Yukon, flew up in a charter."

Hannah said, "After Charlie went up there he called me and said he was worried about my grandfather, so I called Hilda Silva and she made a charter."

Johnny was able to walk out to the plane that had landed on the frozen and snow-covered slough near the cabin. I'm not sure who else was at Gold Camp. I think just Sarah but Maggie and Jimmy Roberts had been there most of the fall. Maybe Sarah asked them to go up and take care of things. Jimmy told me the dog named Grandpa wouldn't leave Gold Camp and that he had to shoot him. That may have been a few days after Johnny left.

During his last few weeks, Johnny had hunted a moose near the cabin, following it off and on for three days. Sometimes the moose was watching Johnny, having come around behind him. "He never even saw it," Sarah chuckled, "getting too old to hunt!"

When he got to the hospital, Doctor Raba said Johnny could still walk but had right-sided weakness. Johnny did not seem to understand English and spoke only in Gwich'in. Hannah said her grandfather recognized people who came to visit and even joked with them. About four or five the next morning he had another stroke and never regained consciousness. After several weeks in the hospital he was transferred to a nursing home. Johnny had pneumonia several times and, as he was no better, the family brought him back to Venetie. Johnny died five days later on December 28, 1977, surrounded by family singing hymns to him.

Sarah said she couldn't worry, that Johnny had lived a long time, always had fun, and that lots of Indian people and white people were his friends.

Stanley said, "Too bad that old man die, huh?" We sat awhile in silence and he added, "Good thing he die so he didn't suffer anymore."

"Yes," I answered. "Even last summer he told me he was ready to go."

There was an increased awareness among us about the fragility of life. A young Fort Yukon man had died in Fairbanks that morning of a broken neck after running into the back of an unlighted truck on his snow machine. Dan Frank had learned that morning of the death of his daughter's one-week-old baby in Nome.

Hannah said, "Nobody knows when they will go."

We sat in silence with that sense being clearly open in our minds. Carl Sandburg's quote came to me, "Nothing surer than death and nothing more unsure than the hour."

"YOU EAT NOW," Sarah said.

I moved over to a table and sat eating.

"Who the hell are you?" someone behind me demanded.

I looked up. It was the stout man I had shared flights with that morning. When I explained my connection with Johnny and Sarah, he seemed to relax and introduced himself, "Jonathon Solomon, Hannah's husband."

When I mentioned I worked for RurAL CAP, Jonathon announced that he was on its board of directors. This led to a discussion of the d-2 bill. The bill proposed expanding the Arctic National Wildlife Range, upgrading it to a wildlife refuge and adding federal wilderness protection of the original portion established in 1960. Another refuge was proposed in the Yukon Flats. I suggested working with the Gwich'in and was shocked to hear Jonathon's abrupt response.

"We don't need any help," he declared. "Don Young is taking care of us. He is married to Lulu, a Gwich'in. He used to teach in Fort Yukon before he was elected to Congress. And no fucking wilderness!"

I had a very different view of Congressman Don Young. My hope of working with the

Gwich'in suddenly seemed distant.

A man came in and was talking quietly with Sarah. I recognized him as the minister from Arctic Village, Trimble Gilbert. It seemed Grandma had sent for him. "Make a dance tonight," she requested.

"Okay, Grandma. We'll send a plane to Arctic Village to get my fiddle."

Word spread quickly. It seemed that planning a dance would have been presumptuous without Sarah's approval. People slowly gathered at the community hall. Musicians tuned their instruments and, just before midnight, Trimble began to play. I stayed with Sarah until she insisted, "Go dance!"

The dance brought a mixture of relief and tears. Maggie and I danced with wet eyes. "Will you still come visit?" she asked.

"Sure," I responded, but I knew it would not be the same without Johnny. My mentor was gone. I could only appreciate the time I had spent with him.

I offered to have a cross and grave marker made. The family agreed on the wording in Gwich'in and English and decided to list Johnny's age as 104, though no one was sure. On his grave marker, Johnny was called the "Father of the Gwich'in Nation, Grandfather of Many."

CHAPTER 21

Caribou Protection

The telephone rang as I entered my office at RurAL CAP on March 14, 1978. One of the issues I followed was the d-2 bill as it evolved through the legislative process. It was my job to inform village councils of significant issues in their region. Then, if they wished, I would arrange a trip to Washington so their representatives could speak at Congressional hearings and meet with committee members.

I picked up the phone.

"Childers here. Have you seen the newspaper this morning?" Bob Childers was a longtime friend and environmentalist.

"No, what's up?"

"The Interior Committee in the House of Representatives voted to open the coastal plain of the Arctic National Wildlife Range to oil and gas exploration."

Incensed, Paul Lowe, Bob Childers, and I met fifteen minutes later to consider the consequences of this development. This area was proposed for federal wilderness protection. It is the calving grounds of the Porcupine caribou herd, named after the Porcupine River.

Bob called the Sierra Club office in Washington, D.C., which played a major role in the Alaska Coalition—a broad network of conservation and other organizations working to pass the d-2 bill, which would protect vast tracts of federal land from development. Bob was told nothing could be done as Representative John Seiberling, a leader for the conservation side, had cut a compromise with Don Young.

"Many of our D.C. team seem to feel they are in charge and that we have nothing to contribute. 'Just stay home and let us take care of it' is their attitude," I said.

"I've thought about how to get this back on the table for discussion," Bob said, pulling maps from his briefcase. "The opinions of the leadership in the concerned villages were left out. Mike, I know from our work together on the Sierra Club executive committee that you have connections in Venetie and Arctic Village. We have to act now. This is the migration pattern of the Porcupine caribou herd," he said as he swept his hand over a vast area on one of the maps. "The proposed area for development is in the heart of the calving grounds. The migrations vary somewhat from year to year but the herd always returns to the coastal plain to calve. This area is free of snow early so nutritious sedges and other grasses are available. The wolves that trail the herd usually stop in the hills to make their dens. Calving takes place in early May before the height of mosquito season."

"So it is habitat that is vital to the health of the herd."

"Exactly."

"I'll also call D.C. to emphasize how important this issue is to Alaskan environmentalists. The next hearing of the d-2 bill is in the House Merchant Marine Committee, not known to be environmentally friendly," Paul offered. As executive director of the Alaska Center for the Environment, Paul Lowe maintained close contact with the decision-makers for the Alaska Coalition.

"I'll go to the Gwich'in villages to let them know about this," I said.

"I'll get pertinent newspaper articles and mark a large map of the Porcupine caribou herd habitat, with the migration routes, the calving grounds, and the area where they approved exploration. The remainder of the Arctic Wildlife Range is designated as wilderness but not the expansion. I'll indicate all that, too." Bob said. "We can put together a package for the villages."

LOCATED IN THE northeast corner of Alaska, the 8.9-million-acre Arctic National Wildlife Range was created in 1960 by an executive order from President Dwight D. Eisenhower. The bill in Congress would expand the range to 19.2 million acres, which would protect the habitat of the Porcupine caribou herd on the U.S. side of the border. Much of the herd's winter range was in Canada where it was basically undisturbed except for the Dempster Highway between Dawson City in the Yukon and Fort McPherson in the Northwest Territories. Gwich'in villages and the Inuit village of Kaktovik on opposite edges of the wildlife range were dependent on the caribou for their food. In the Gwich'in villages, hunting and fishing provided most of the nutrition and, when combined with firewood gathering, was essentially a full-time job.

I returned to RurAL CAP and called Jonathon Solomon, whom I had met at Johnny's funeral. "Jonathon, the House Interior Committee voted to open the coastal calving grounds of the Porcupine herd to oil and gas exploration. It's in the morning paper. This is the first we've heard of it. I plan to go to the villages to let them know."

"No way!" he said. "Don Young met with us a few days ago in Fairbanks and told us everything was taken care of."

"I can bring the articles and maps to explain it," I said, resisting the temptation to say that it appeared Don Young had "taken care" of them.

"Okay, you come here first," he grumbled. Jonathon was a traditional Gwich'in leader. In addition to being active in RurAL CAP, he served on the board of Doyon, Ltd., the regional Native corporation created for interior Alaska by the Alaska Native Claims Settlement Act. He had been mayor of Fort Yukon, too. Jonathon's opinion would be important.

Next I called Jim Kowalsky in Fairbanks. Jim, the Alaska representative for Friends of the Earth, was a strong and vocal supporter of a subsistence priority for Natives. Most environmental conservation organizations were unaware of the subsistence issue or didn't care about it.

"Jim, can you go with me to Fort Yukon and the Gwich'in villages? Guess you have seen the morning paper."

"Sure, I can go anytime. I was alarmed to see that article this morning."

"Good," I said. "Paul Lowe and Bob Childers are gathering information and drafting a letter of protest for the Alaskan environmental groups to sign. The Alaska Coalition people in D.C. say it is a done deal. I suspect they traded for an overall increase in acreage. They are discouraging anyone from going back to fight it."

Several days later, Jim and I met Jonathon at the Fort Yukon airstrip. The ground was covered with snow; it was dark and the temperature was thirty-five below.

"Where are you staying? The hotel is closed," Jonathon announced gruffly.

"We can go to the old Hudson Stuck Hospital. They usually have room there."

"Give me the papers," he said. "I'll take you over there."

I handed Jonathon a package of articles Bob and I had gathered from several sources. We had copied thirty sets at RurAL CAP.

Jonathon called me an hour later. "Be ready at first light," he said, anger in his voice. "I chartered a plane. We're going to the villages! Fucking Don Young told us everything was okay!"

We flew to Venetie the next morning. Jonathon notified the tribal chief and soon we gathered with elders and the village council in a small log home. I thought Jonathon would take over but he nodded to me and said, "Well, explain the situation to them."

Fortunately I knew most of the people, but introduced Jim Kowalsky and myself as we handed out copies of the news articles. On a log wall I pinned the large map Bob had prepared. "You know more about the caribou than I do but let me review their migration routes and the areas they use."

I gave a summary of the issue and explained the legislative process underway in Washington. "So if the d-2 bill passes like this, there will be oil exploration and development in this area, called the '1002' area."

A long discussion in Gwich'in followed. Finally I lay down on the floor and napped while the elders talked for several hours. They knew this area and felt it to be sacred. The 1002 area was in the heart of the caribou calving grounds. Their conclusion was unanimous: Oil development there would be a threat to the caribou. It had long been Gwich'in philosophy that the caribou were not to be hunted or disturbed in their "nursery."

"We have a spiritual connection with the caribou," one of the elders explained. "As long as the herd is healthy, the Gwich'in will be healthy. We know the calving grounds even though we live far from it. Long ago one man always want to know where the caribou go, so finally he follow them for a few years. Some of our people used to live on the north side of the mountains above Arctic Village. They knew that place, too. If they disturb the caribou in that area it will hurt the caribou and the Gwich'in."

A resolution to this effect was drawn up and signed. Maggie Roberts was chosen by the Venetie council to accompany us.

The four of us flew to Arctic Village, one of the most picturesque places in Alaska. It was twenty-five below but calm. The sky was deep blue. The snow was rose-tinted from the low sun. Mountains rose to the north and west. Hills rolled eastward. Spring in the Arctic!

In Arctic Village, the process was much the same as in Venetie, with the same conclusion: Disturbance of the calving area would be detrimental to the health of the herd and would violate a sacred place. The Arctic Village Council members wrote and signed a resolution to that effect. They designated Trimble Gilbert to go with us.

"Now we have to go to Old Crow," Jonathon declared.

"That's the Yukon Territory. We can't go to Canada!" I exclaimed.

"We have to let Old Crow people know what is happening and get their support," Jonathon said. "They are Gwich'in, too."

Jonathon's father had run a freight barge on the Porcupine River from Fort Yukon to Old Crow for many years. Jonathon frequently went with him and had kept in touch with friends and relatives on that side of the international boundary.

Jim Kowalsky returned to Fairbanks. We went on to Old Crow. A general meeting was called and once again Jonathon said, "Okay, give the overall view." The decision was the same: The calving grounds must be protected.

"Jonathon, we've got to go to Kaktovik now."

"I'm not going to a fucking Eskimo village! You go."

I had never been to Kaktovik before. Unlike the Gwich'in villages with their Native tribal governments, Kaktovik was classified as a second-class city under state law. During the next three days I went from home to home visiting the city council members. On the first round I introduced myself, explained why I was there, and showed the Gwich'in resolutions. Every one of the council members encouraged me to draft a resolution against development in the 1002 area. On the second round I reviewed the draft with each council member and drank a lot of tea and coffee. On the third round, when everyone was satisfied with the wording, they signed the resolution.

SEVERAL DAYS LATER, I sat on the lawn of the Capitol Building in Washington, D.C. among daffodils and cherry blossoms. The grass was green. The contrast to the previous week seemed unreal. Jonathon, Trimble Gilbert, Clara Gundrum, and I were there for the d-2 hearing in the House Merchant Marine Committee. They were to testify as representatives of their villages. The committee chairman, Lloyd Jones, favored oil development.

As Clara and I walked down a hallway on the way to the hearing room, someone approached us from behind and grasped her shoulder. She turned, smiled, and started to say hello.

Don Young interrupted, "What are you doing here?" His voice was harsh. He was not pleased to learn why she had come to Washington.

Jonathon elegantly and without hesitation testified first, then Clara and Trimble. On arrival in Washington we'd gone to the Sierra Club office to meet Alaska Coalition leaders and lobbyists. Jack Hession, the Sierra Club's Alaska staff representative, repeated the message given us by phone: "It's no use; it's a done deal." No encouragement came from any of the coalition environmentalists. Several expressed surprise that we believed it was such an important issue. The Alaska Coalition leaders reluctantly spent a few minutes with the Gwich'in delegates. I apologized to my companions for the rude reception.

After the hearing we assembled in Congressman Don Young's office. I remained in the outer reception area while the others joined him. Clara was related to Don's wife, and was invited to stay with the two of them, though she was miffed at the Congressman's behavior earlier in the hall. Framed photos of Johnny and Sarah were on the wall, taken by Bruce Dale of National Geographic. I was studying them when Clara stuck her head out of the back office. "Don Young wants to talk with you."

Nervously I entered. I was still on the Alaska Sierra Club executive committee and knew Young had no love for environmentalists.

"Who are you?" he demanded.

"I used to stay with Johnny and Sarah at Gold Camp. They are my son's godparents. I'm now working for RurAL CAP as a subsistence advocate."

"Why in the hell is RurAL CAP involved in this?" Young asked.

Jonathon spoke, "It's okay. I'm on the board. We just cannot let development occur in the calving grounds, Don." Jonathon was direct but cordial as he represented his peoples' views.

After a half-hour discussion, Don Young said, "Well, it's not going to make a lot of people happy but we'll pull the 1002 provision out of the bill."

Delighted, we informed leaders in the Alaska Coalition of Young's promise. They were unanimous in their cynicism and expressed disbelief that this would happen. There were no words of encouragement, support, or congratulations for what the Gwich'in delegation had accomplished.

The 1002 area was dropped quietly from the mark-up of the House bill. Language to open the coastal plain to petroleum exploration would reappear later in the Senate version, becoming the most debated section of the bill. Jonathon was a leader in the fight to protect the Porcupine caribou herd's calving grounds, even traveling to Kaktovik several times.

The d-2 bill, formally the Alaska National Interest Lands Conservation Act, was signed into law by President Carter in 1980. The act established ninety-seven million acres of new or expanded parks and wildlife refuges and protected subsistence hunting, giving a rural priority to harvest fish and game. The bill also required studies of the 1002 area, the calving grounds of the Porcupine caribou herd. Seismic testing helped define oil potential. The controversy grew. It became the top issue for the major environmental groups. More villages in Alaska and Canada, dependent upon the herd, became involved. The Gwich'in continue to advocate for protection of the calving grounds.

CHAPTER 22

Sarah's Memories

The sky was clear, warm, and bright blue on a day in late April 1980. The ground was muddy, but drying fast. It was an easy breakup. In Venetie it was spring-cleaning time. I was staying at Stanley's.

I had finally met a professional interested in recording Sarah's memories, and we were here to interview her. Bill Schneider was an anthropologist with the Alaska Native Language Center in Fairbanks. Because Sarah spoke little English, we decided to record her in Gwich'in with Maggie giving intermittent summaries in English.

"William Loola was the first Native preacher," Sarah began. "He married Johnny and me at Fort Yukon in 1907.

"I had been to Fort Yukon once before. Maybe I was eight years old. That winter we ran out of food. Many people left. Some went to Old Crow and others to Fort Yukon. One day my father returned home to Old John Lake. There were no animals, so he said, 'Let's go down toward Yukon Flats area.'

"We traveled by dog team. We traveled without eating. The poor dogs were just barely walking. My father went ahead to Fort Yukon and two dog teams came for us. That was first time I had ever seen crackers, flour, sugar, tea—cloth pants, too. They sure look funny to me.

"When we got to Fort Yukon we saw our first white men. There were just a few living around there. We were really scared of them so we stayed out of their sight."

After they married, Sarah and Johnny lived in Fort Yukon for a while. Then they went up the East Fork of the Chandalar with her parents, to Old John Lake.

"Our first baby, Lucy, was born at Old John Lake. Then we moved down to Otter Creek for a long time. We made a cabin there. Quite a few people lived at Otter Creek then but there was no chief. The caribou came by there. Everybody helped each other.

"We still moved around a lot with a canvas tent and a little stove. Mostly we used meat, not much flour, rice or tea. If somebody went to Fort Yukon for food they had to pack it back in summer or use dog team in winter. We stayed at Otter Creek until we had three children. After that we moved north to the Koness River. We lived there for twenty-five years."

Sarah said Arctic Village did not exist at that time. She and Johnny and another man built the first cabin there. Later Johnny and Sarah moved to Gold Camp.

"He dreamed about that place and we moved down there. We went down the river in a skin boat. That was my first time in a skin boat but I was not scared. Maybe a little bit when there were big rocks in the river. That was 1934.

"Maggie was born in 1935 at Fort Yukon. There was no one to help at Gold Camp so my son Nathaniel went down with me with a dog team while Johnny stayed in Gold Camp with the kids."

Sarah told stories about times when food was scarce. Then she was ready to rest.

I visited around the village, drinking tea at every stop. Paul Tritt was home. I always went to see if he needed repair of one of his well-used prosthetic arms. Paul's left arm had been amputated just below the elbow years before due to a tumor.

"*Neenjit doonch'yaa,*" we greeted one another. "Come in, drink tea," he invited.

As we sat, I examined the amputated stump. What remained of his own arm had healed well. He play-boxed with it. "I shot a moose this winter."

"How do you hold the rifle steady?" I asked.

Paul laughed, "I prop it on tree limb. One shot, I knock him down!" He brought out two prostheses. Both had home repairs with wire and tape. The "hooks" were the type for heavy tool use. "I use chain saw, everything! Did you check my records?"

"Yes. The cancer was a fibrosarcoma. There is no sign of it coming back. Tell me again what happened."

"Well, remember, maybe twenty-five years ago I was setting a trap. I hear a little noise, just like brush move but no wind. I look up and just on other side of willow is big wolf, maybe that far!" He pointed to a chair six feet away. "I was kneeling so I'm looking him right in the eyes. He jumped at me and I threw up my left arm. He chew it pretty bad and then run away! I clean my arm good with snow and wrap it up. It heal okay and no problem for maybe eighteen or twenty years, then start to grow that cancer."

I told Paul I would take his "arms" to Anchorage for repair.

• • •

THE NEXT MORNING I kneeled on the floor with Dan Frank and Abraham Christian looking at maps. They conversed with Sarah in Gwich'in and showed me the places she had talked about the day before. Bill Schneider arrived, then Maggie. Several young people joined us to listen.

"Dan was the youngest at the time of no food that I tell you yesterday," Sarah told us. "For those first three kids I use moss for diaper, change it every time they pee. Work good. After that, used cloth rags somebody send up from Fort Yukon. Those Fort Yukon people help me lots with clothes, sewing kit. I send them piece of tanned skin. Tan lots of skins in my life. When Maggie was little she wore all fur and skin clothes.

"Some of my children die of tuberculosis. Most of them had it. Before white people come, not much sickness. Then there was sickness with throat problem, too, that hit mostly young people. Later came the flu. It hit everybody, old people, too. Used to be people had good teeth but since people eat sugar and candy get toothache and sores. I never eat candy as a kid. That why my teeth are good.

"Even when we had bad time we take care of old women. We took care of four old women. We even hauled them around in toboggan in wintertime. I even carry them on my back. Across the rocks on the mountain I cut two sticks to help keep my balance. Heavy! We just go a little way and camp.

"Johnny helped build the first school in Venetie. That was 1936 before the government school. Johnny was visiting and worked with Ned Roberts, Elijah John, and others to fix up a little cabin. They chose Hannah Stevens to be the teacher. They pay her some with money from fur they trap. After one year John Fredson came. He wanted to be teacher for his own people so he came with his wife and their two kids."

I knew that John Fredson had arrived in the fall of 1937 to find only two children in the village. He encouraged families to settle in Venetie so the school would have an enrollment of at least thirteen students, the minimum required for a government-supported Bureau of Indian Affairs school.

Fredson was Gwich'in and spoke his Native language fluently. His mother had died in childbirth. When Fredson was seven, his father Old Fred took him to Circle to live with Lizzie Woods, an Episcopal mission teacher. Several years later Lizzie and her husband moved to Fort Yukon where she taught school. From time to time Old Fred took John out into the country to teach him Gwich'in ways.

Archdeacon Stuck, the Episcopal missionary, recognized Fredson's brilliance and chose him to support his team of climbers who made the first successful ascent of Mount McKinley in 1913. John, then fourteen, took care of the base camp while the others climbed. Walter Harper, whose mother was Gwich'in, had the honor of being the first to stand on the summit.

Fredson later accompanied Stuck throughout northern Alaska, traveling by boat, the *Pelican,* in summer and by dog sled in winter. Under Stuck's sponsorship, John finished high school in Vermont and then earned a degree at Stuck's alma mater, Sewanee, the University of the South, in Tennessee.

Later Fredson returned to Fort Yukon where he worked in the Northern Commercial Company store. In 1932, he married Jean Ribaloff, an Aleut nurse working at the hospital there.

Fredson came to Venetie at a critical time. With his Western education and knowledge, he understood the complex federal requirements for reservation status. On January 1, 1938, Fredson wrote a letter requesting establishment of a reservation. First a constitution had to be written and adopted and a tribal council elected to serve three-year terms. Fredson wrote the constitution. Johnny Frank traveled by dog team in the winter of 1939 to scattered Gwich'in camps throughout the region, including Arctic Village and Wind River. He obtained the necessary signatures to approve the constitution and to elect a tribal government. In May 1943, the federal government formally established the Venetie Indian Reservation, one of few approved in Alaska. Johnny was the first chief. The women selected Sarah to represent them as the first women's chief.

ON OUR THIRD DAY of recording, Sarah began, "When John Fredson came to be the first teacher at the government school, there was not much food. Hunting was not good and people were having a hard time." She and Johnny had enough food to last the winter in Gold Camp until Johnny gave away some of the food and later they ran out themselves. Then they moved with their seven children to Venetie to help keep the school open. By the end of 1937 there were twenty-four students and eighty-nine people living in the village. That's when John and Johnny began thinking about a reservation for Gwich'in country.

While Sarah was talking, Abraham Christian came in. We rose and everyone chatted. I walked with Abraham to his cabin. Annie was home and smiled as she greeted me. I sat for tea. Like everyone else, they had moved up onto the bluff. As usual Abraham didn't talk much.

Sarah was ready to resume when Maggie and I arrived the next morning. She seemed to be happy that her stories were important to us. Maggie sat holding her mother's hand as Bill Schneider got the recorder ready.

Maggie told her, "We want to know more about the reservation. Why did you want it? How did you know about reservations?"

"Well, we read in the Bible that there would be too many people," Sarah said. "We wanted to protect our land where we fished and hunted and trapped ... We got the idea after hearing about people claiming reservations in the Lower 48. We heard about Fairbanks and trouble there."

"Were you afraid that the land would not be given to you?" Bill asked.

"Yes. We were afraid this place would be swarming with people and that it would be hard to get around. We got the reservation because we were thinking that would happen. I see my own grandchildren and other people have a hard time getting around in Fairbanks because it's so overcrowded, right? We thought if we had a reservation, we wouldn't be like Fairbanks.

"John Fredson told Johnny that there were reservations down in the Lower 48. They both wanted to do the same thing here ... so they both went to work on it. John wrote a letter and everyone signed the papers. They tried to get all the signatures. After everyone signed up here, Johnny went to Arctic Village with one of our boys. He told the people there and they signed. Chief Christian and some people were living at Wind River so he went there, too. They signed up and then he came back. That was wintertime and he went up by dog team.

"After they got the reservation, people were jealous of good job Johnny did and they kicked him out as chief. Then we went back to Gold Camp."

The Venetie Reservation was smaller than the area traditionally used by the Gwich'in. It left out lands between the east and middle forks of the Chandalar River, which included Gold Camp. Alaska Natives could personally acquire title of up to one hundred sixty acres of federal land. Johnny did so to protect Gold Camp.

Sarah continued, "A man from Washington, D.C. came to Gold Camp for this reservation. Johnny worked to get the reservation and then he built a house outside the reservation boundary, you see. And we lived there ...

"When the man first came into the house, he set his papers down and shook hands with us. Then he said, 'Why did you make a reservation and then build outside the reservation?'

"Your father pointed to him and said, 'So you will not take away all the land that surrounds me.'"

CHAPTER 23

Margie

Although telephones and television had arrived in Venetie, neither were available at my mountain cabin near Anchorage. In 1979, I'd returned to part-time work at the Native hospital. After several difficult years of separation, in 1982 my marriage to Elizabeth was over. I was involved in a new relationship with Margie Gibson and brought her north to meet my Gwich'in family. Margie and I had met during the "d-2 days" when she was Alaska representative for Friends of the Earth. She was my height and slender, with long blond hair framing a narrow face. Round wire-rimmed glasses added to her serious expression. She was intelligent and decisive.

In October 1983, Margie and I sat in Grandma Sarah's house. A coloring-book cutout pinned on the wall drew my attention. It depicted Plymouth Rock and the arrival of the Mayflower in 1620. Two pilgrims stood on the beach, grinning broadly. This was so ironic. American Indians had suffered many setbacks and loss of their lands and independence since then.

The morning was bright and mild, the mud and ground barely freezing, and the frost was melting from the roof. Ravens sailed by to land on the peak of Dan Frank's cabin roof where they pecked at the foam recently used to seal the spaces between the logs.

Grandma sat quietly, her essentially blind eyes closed, using a toothpick, occasionally spitting tobacco juice into a can from her usual after-breakfast treat of Black Bull twist tobacco. "I can't quit it even if I don't want it sometime," Sarah laughed. She told me she had known I was coming, and mentioned this to Maggie, though I had not contacted her or anyone else in the village.

Sarah's dress was brown velveteen, made for her birthday potlatch the previous week. Two new walking canes leaned against the wall. She showed me new scarves and a beaded tobacco pouch. Forty to fifty people had come from Arctic Village, Fort Yukon, Fairbanks, and elsewhere.

"I was feeling bad before they came. The gathering made me feel good. All bad go out!" she said, making a sweeping motion over her body.

The potlatch honored her 101st birthday. Her grandson Stanley and several other men had gone up the East Fork to Wind River where they killed a moose. Sarah showed me Polaroid photos of the party and a dance that followed.

We visited Stanley at his cabin. "We don't visit much anymore now that there is TV and telephones. We just stay home," Stanley told us. He was living with Elizabeth Martinez, whose husband had been killed some years before in an auto accident. Her two children were playing Pac-Man, a computer game. They were adept. After much encouragement, we tried it. At first the children thought our feeble attempts were to tease them, but when they realized this was our skill level, they laughed so hard they rolled on the floor.

We watched the television news, which was relayed to rural Alaska on a satellite system. I thought how Johnny would have liked to have seen footage from around the world. He always listened to the radio news carefully and formed his own views on world issues, sometimes integrated with the Bible. He associated Republicans with the Pharisees of biblical days, explaining how they cared only for themselves.

Outside, the sky was ablaze with northern lights as tentacles of green and pink shot across the sky. I wondered if Johnny had returned there.

At Maggie's, the ever-present television blared in the background as she played cards with her daughters Sylvia and Melody and a few others. Then we stopped to see Jessie Williams. Jessie's husband, Albert, had died and her sister Clara was living with her. Clara's legs were paralyzed following a spinal cord injury from a snow-machine accident. She was beading, sitting in a wheelchair.

When her favorite TV show, *Dallas,* came on, Clara announced, "Okay, be quiet now for this program!" I tried to joke with her but she was serious.

Mary Medford, Hannah Solomon's sister, was staying for six months to help care for Grandma Sarah. Lawrence Roberts, who ran a flying service, Gwich'in Air, had given a little frame house to his grandma and she was glad to be in her own home. The freezer was full of grayling, moose, and caribou. A large supply of firewood was stacked in the yard. While Mary beaded a beautiful pair of moose-skin mittens, she talked openly of her problems with alcohol, blood pressure, thyroid, and nerves. She was happy to be in Venetie now that the village had voted itself dry.

Steven Peter of Arctic Village came in. Steven was seventy-seven but looked fifty. He was an Episcopal lay minister and had come to spend time with Sarah.

"You know why white people get gray hair young?" Steven asked, and then answered his own question. "It's because of their diet. Old people used not to have gray hair eating fresh meat—moose, sheep, caribou, fish, ground squirrel, and rabbit. Now there is too much white-man food, store food, and alcohol, too. I used to drink but I gave it up." He made a motion with his hand of brushing alcohol aside. "Alcohol makes the blood thin, too. No good."

I had to agree that many store foods were unhealthy, including white flour, sugars, white rice, highly refined carbohydrates, and fried foods.

ONE DAY FIVE YEARS later, Maggie called to tell me that Grandma was in the hospital in Fairbanks.

"What happened? Who sent her?"

"Jessie. She fell against the wood stove and burn her leg. It got infection."

I phoned the floor nurse at Fairbanks Memorial Hospital and inquired about Sarah.

"She has a large burn, mostly second degree, a hand-sized area on the lateral thigh. It is cleaning up but it looked pretty bad when she came in a few days ago. Social service will check out the home situation."

"Why social service?"

"To check for elder abuse."

I was shocked. "Please transfer me to social service. I know the family well and can vouch that this is not abuse."

"Okay, but the burn looked neglected."

I called Maggie. "Grandma is okay but they want to put her in Denali Center, the nursing home, in a few days. Her doctor wants her to stay until the wound is completely healed."

I flew to Fairbanks the morning of May 5, 1988, and went straight to the Andrew Isaac Health Center, where I was directed to the nearby nursing home. It was a dark and depressing place but the staff was pleasant and caring.

Sarah was sitting in an overstuffed recliner chair facing away from the door. I stood watching her a moment. She looked forlorn, unmoving, and unfocused. She had been essentially blind the past few years in Venetie after a cataract operation went bad. She lost all vision in one eye. She still had a little vision in the other eye and was reluctant to have further surgery. Finally she had moved in with Maggie. One of the many little "camp robbers," as she loved to call her great-grandchildren, had bumped into her, causing her to fall against the wood stove.

I greeted her in Gwich'in.

"Who is that?" she asked, holding my face close.

"Mike Holloway, Grandma."

"Here?"

"Yes, Grandma, I came to see you." I sat down beside her and encouraged her to eat the soup a student nurse was trying to feed her.

Fortunately, Hannah Bundschuh, one of Sarah's granddaughters, worked at the nursing home and came in to translate. "She talks about how good it is to see you and asks you to help her go home. She can't walk since she fell about a month ago but her hip doesn't hurt much anymore. I'm the only one who can talk to her. Nobody else speaks Gwich'in. She is lonely for home."

I sat holding Sarah's hand for a while. Her burn had healed. One glance and I knew she had broken her hip, which I discovered later had resulted from a fall at the nursing home. Her right leg was shortened and the foot rotated out.

I reviewed Sarah's medical record, including her x-ray. Her right hip was not included on the x-ray of her thighbone. Grandma's fall was recorded but a note said "No fracture." Her doctor was out of town for a week.

I told Hannah, "Please tell Grandma that we'll get her home soon. I'll call Maggie."

"MAGGIE." It still seemed odd to be able to phone her. "I went to see Grandma. Her burn is healed. She wants to come home. I think that she should."

"We told the doctor, but he said she wasn't ready."

"When she fell in the nursing home last month she broke her hip."

"Hannah told us they said no fracture."

"With her age and weak bone, they wouldn't operate anyway but there is no x-ray of her hip, only part of the thigh bone."

A week later I was in surgery when Jonathon Soloman called. When I called him back, he got right to the point, as usual. "Call that doctor and tell him to send Grandma Sarah home."

I called.

"They just can't take care of her there," the doctor said. "The family neglected her. Besides, Medicare doesn't have money just now for non-emergency travel and she would have to charter."

"She wants to go home. You know her hip is broken."

"The x-ray didn't show a fracture."

"It didn't show her hip. Have you seen her? Her right leg is shortened and externally rotated. She cannot walk."

"Well, she'll die if she goes home."

"She is over one hundred years old, is blind, can't walk, and in a strange dark place where she can't communicate. She wants to go home to die!" I hung up and called Jonathon.

"Jonathon, her doctor won't discharge her."

Jonathon told me, "Call him back and tell him that if Grandma doesn't get home right away, we will sue him for neglect and not knowing that she had a broken hip."

I called after my next surgery and related Jonathon's message, though in a less colorful way. Sarah flew on a charter to Venetie with a medical escort two days later.

Two weeks later, Margie and I sat at Sarah's bedside. Maggie had made a bed for her in the big front room so she could visit with everyone. I held her hand. She greeted us warmly and thanked us for coming to visit. Her face radiated peace. She was the essence of calm. Her grandkids and great-grandkids played quietly nearby, stopping now and then at her bed. Visitors dropped by and sat with her awhile in near silence. Maggie brushed Grandma's hair and brought her tea.

I told Sarah we were going to Arctic Village to attend the first gathering of the Gwich'in in perhaps a century. Afterward we would come down the river in our kayak and visit again. She nodded, but I think we each knew this was our last visit. Tears filled my eyes as we walked away.

THE GATHERING IN Arctic Village, *Gwich'in Niintsyaa* (literally "Where We Feast"), was organized to promote the need for protection of the caribou calving grounds but it and subsequent gatherings had a much broader effect. This caribou issue, so important to the Gwich'in, grew into a revitalization movement uniting people across the region from northeastern Alaska to the western Northwest Territories.

Gwich'in Niintsyaa was held in the new community hall completed at 3:30 a.m. the opening day of the gathering. About forty feet by one hundred feet, the hall was built of upright logs with eight large windows. It was filled with Gwich'in people from across the Arctic. The population of this village of 125 people had doubled. Some guests camped but most were taken into homes, and everyone was fed.

Elders gathered near the front of the hall, renewing old friendships or being introduced. Voices blended in a low, gentle hum. There were no loud or acrimonious sounds. Trimble Gilbert arrived wearing an Episcopal smock, collar, and robe to give the opening prayer. An hour before I had seen him returning from checking his fish net, dressed in river clothes, carrying a whitefish. Transformed, he welcomed everyone, informing us that the last such Gwich'in gathering had taken place on the Colleen River a century before.

Most of the meeting was an open session. One by one people rose to talk about the joy of gathering together. They discussed problems threatening them: alcoholism, loss of cultural ways, the importance of keeping their language alive, and, as always, the importance of caribou and the need to protect their birthing area and nursery.

On the last day, resolutions were adopted unanimously supporting protection of the Porcupine caribou herd calving grounds through a federal wilderness designation. The Gwich'in Steering Committee was established to work for caribou protection. Among those chosen to be on the committee were the passionate orators Jonathon Solomon of Fort Yukon, Sarah James of Arctic Village, and Norma Kassi of Old Crow. Bob Childers was appointed a consultant to the committee.

After the gathering, Edward Sam, my "sister" Jenny Sam's son, took Margie and me up the Junjik River in his boat. The water level was high, flooding the low areas. We camped for several days. One morning, Edward told us, "Gee, I sure don't like to come up here with those old women!"

"Why?" I asked, surprised.

"They say, 'Look, I see sheep!' I look all around. I don't see sheep. 'Up there, on mountain.' I look. On far mountain, I see little white dots. 'Too far,' I tell them. They start to talk about how good sheep taste, how they never eat sheep in long time and best way to fix it. They just keep on until finally I pick up my rifle and go hunt sheep."

Edward returned downriver. Margie and I stayed, putting our folding kayak together a few days later, packing and starting down the Chandalar. We had planned to float the East Fork to Venetie but stopped at Arctic Village. As we pulled in to the bank, a boy approached and said, "They said to tell you to go to Venetie. Grandma Sarah Frank die this morning."

We caught a flight and were there in a few hours. We went directly to Maggie's house.

"I was just sitting with her, holding her hand when she passed away quietly," Maggie said. "I'm glad you come. I thought maybe you already start downriver. Go with me to church. We make her new slippers."

Sarah lay in an open coffin. Maggie's eyes flooded with tears as she started to put beautiful new beaded moccasins on Grandma's stocking-covered feet. Maggie looked at me, and I took the moccasins from her and pulled them into place.

"Put her prayer book in her hands," she requested, holding it out to me.

I crossed Sarah's hands on her chest, gently placing the thoroughly worn old book in hands that had worked so many years through so many hardships. This remarkable old woman had seen ten of her children die and had survived famines herself, yet never became embittered.

Sarah was buried beside Johnny. This time I was content to stand with Margie as the grave was filled. I shook my head when offered a shovel.

Epilogue

I still visit Gwich'in country but not so often these days. No one lives in Gold Camp now. It is returning to the earth.

Maggie Frank Roberts passed away in December 2013, at the age of 78. She was at home in Venetie. We stayed in touch through the years as she continued to raise new generations of children. I'd receive calls off and on, especially when she was worried about some young Gwich'in arriving in Anchorage. Maggie was active in the tribal council for many years, and a mentor to many. Her kind, quiet influence will live on in all who knew her. Her brothers, Nathaniel, Hamel, and Dan have passed on, as have Jimmy Roberts, Stanley Frank, Abraham Christian, Jenny and Moses Sam, Jessie Williams, Clara Gundrum, and Jonathon Solomon.

Lawrence Roberts operated his own small plane charter business, Gwich'in Air, for some years before getting into the construction industry where he became a supervisor. He remarried after a divorce with Mary Rose and now lives near Fairbanks.

Kenneth Frank, a grandson of Johnny and Sarah, and his wife, Caroline Tritt Frank, work, teach, and preserve Gwich'in language, genealogy, philosophy, and history. They have a home in Arctic Village. Both have university degrees. They have two daughters. Kenneth calls periodically, and we visit each other occasionally.

Many Gwich'in the age of Johnny and Sarah's grandchildren are active on Facebook and I stay in touch with them there.

My brother Ted Holloway became a medical doctor and had a thirty-year career as district public health director in southern Georgia. He was very active in HIV/AIDS prevention and treatment. He still lives there with his wife, Linda. Their daughter, her husband, and two grandsons are next door. After our 1962 trip to Gwich'in country, Ted returned twice to visit Venetie and Arctic Village.

Bill Bennett retired after a career as a family doctor in rural South Carolina and is writing a book about his early adventures.

Richard Volkwein became a commercial pilot with United Airlines. He retired with his wife, Jean, to Tennessee.

Willy Carpenter became a gynecologist and obstetrician in private practice in South Carolina.

Bob Childers continues to be involved with the Gwich'in Steering Committe and conservation organizations to protect the Porcupine caribou calving grounds.

Elizabeth and I divorced in 1982. She completed doctoral studies in psychology for a career in counseling. She lives in British Columbia, a few hours from our son and his family.

My son, David Holloway, has a doctorate in chemistry and applies it to research and teaching at the British Columbia Institute of Technology in Burnaby, Canada, where he lives with his wife, Marilyn, and daughters, Mikayla and Lauren.

Margie Gibson worked with environmental groups and Native communities in Alaska for many years. By the time we married in 1997 we had made many trips together to Gwich'in country.

During my work for habitat protection and a subsistence hunting and fishing priority for those who live with the land, I was "following my bliss," as Joseph Campbell would say. I worked with a single-mindedness to protect the unique rural Alaska way of life and preserve vast areas of wilderness habitat.

The Gwich'in and many other groups and organizations have been successfully protecting the calving grounds of the Porcupine caribou. The herd remains healthy.

I worked at Alaska Native Medical Center as an orthopedic surgeon until diagnosed with Parkinson's disease in 2001. In the decade following, I taught orthopedics in Africa, Central America, and Asia with Health Volunteers Overseas, accompanied by Margie. We continue to support those programs.

Like Johnny Frank, these days a narrow band of silver rings my brown eyes.

Johnny and Sarah Frank had a profound effect on my life. I have attempted in the years of writing this book to capture something of their essence so that their influence might in some way continue and help others, as they always helped others in life. They lived a hard life, yet were always generous. Johnny and Sarah lived in harmony with the land and were at peace with themselves.

Acknowledgments

This story is based upon my journals, notes, letters, recordings and memories. I wrote the first chapters over thirty years ago and set them aside to return to fixing bones until the onset of Parkinson's disease gave me the time to resume. Over the years family and friends encouraged me to try to capture this story of friendship between a young Southern white boy and two Arctic Gwich'in elders and how it influenced our lives and events. I respectfully edited conversations and stories for clarity.

Mahsi'choo to Nathaniel Frank, Hamel Frank, Dan Frank, Maggie Frank Roberts and their families for their acceptance and hospitality, as well as to many others in Venetie; to Chief Abraham Christian and his wife Annie Christian for their kindness and guidance; to Stanley Frank for graciously leading us overland to his grandparents Johnny and Sarah Frank on the East Fork of the Chandalar River; and to Richard and Mildred Birchell for their hospitality. A special *Mahsi'choo* to my "sister" Maggie Roberts for her continued friendship through the years.

I am indebted to my parents for their love and confidence, allowing me to take my younger brother Ted beyond the end of the road and into the Alaskan wilderness.

Richard Volkwein and Ted photographed our first experiences in Gwich'in country and kindly gave permission to include their photos in this book. Ted spent many hours restoring and scanning the original slides, read two manuscript drafts, and offered steady support. Thanks to Kenneth Frank and Craig Mischler for reviewing an early draft and offering encouragement and advice as well as help with Gwich'in words.

It is impossible to properly acknowledge my gratitude to my wife, Margie Gibson, for her steady support in writing this book, as well as typing, editing, and organizing. She also designed the book cover and maps.

Margie and I appreciate the support of our friends who helped in so many ways, from reading early drafts of the manuscript to fixing us dinner, including Gordon Wright, Bob and Dorothy Childers, Art Davidson, Jan Flanders, Richard Ibarguen, Jill Fredson, Carol Wilson, Frances Penvenne, Steve Westby, Veronique de Jaegher, and Bill Lindenau.

To Nancy Stockdale for her editing skills goes a special thanks.

My final thanks in the production of this book goes to Epicenter Press. Acquisitions editor Lael Morgan encouraged me to persist in rewriting my manuscript, even if my initial submission made her "head ache and want to fall off." She was a steady source of support in a long and, for a first time author, somewhat murky process. The editing skills of publisher Kent Sturgis helped shape the story.

. . .

Author's Notes

Any profits I receive from this book will benefit the Gwich'in through programs such as the Johnny and Sarah Frank Educational Fund at the University of Alaska Fairbanks and the Gwich'in Steering Committee.

Maggie Roberts worked with Bill Schneider to record Sarah's stories for the Alaska Native Language Center. Later, Johnny and Sarah's surviving children Nathaniel, Hamel, Dan and Maggie worked with Craig Mishler, an ethnologist, Ron Frank, a grandson, and many others to locate and preserve the numerous scattered recordings of the stories of Johnny and Sarah in Gwich'in, which captured the details and nuances that so add to their richness. These were then translated by Mary Rose Roberts, Judy Erick, and Lillian Garnett, edited by Craig Mishler and published in a book by the Alaska Native Language Center in *Neerihiinjik: We Traveled From Place to Place*. I highly recommend it to those who wish to learn more about the lives of Johnny and Sarah Frank.